ASSASSIN'S CREED™

2 | AQUILUS

STORY : CORBEYRAN
ART : DJILLALI DEFALI
COLOR : ALEXIS SENTENAC

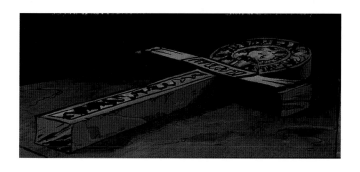

ASSASSIN'S CREED: AQUILUS

ISBN: 9781781163412

Published by Titan Books
A division of Titan Publishing Group Ltd.
144 Southwark St.
London
SE1 0UP

First Titan edition: October 2012
English-language translation: Mark McKenzie-Ray

10 9 8 7 6 5 4 3 2

Printed in the United States of America

What did you think of this book? We love to hear from our readers. Please email us
at: readerfeedback@titanemail.com, or write to us at the above address. To receive
advance information, news, competitions, and exclusive offers online, please sign up
for the Titan newsletter on our website: www.titanbooks.com

ACKNOWLEDGMENTS

Thank you to Djillali Defali for setting me on this fascinating adventure. To Alexis Nolent for being
my guide and accompanying me through this new territory. Thanks also to François Tallec, Olivier
Henriot and Geoffroy Sardi, as well as the teams at Ubisoft Paris and Montreal, for opening their
doors and welcoming me into this universe.

CORBEYRAN

Thank you to Matz for the phone call, even if you regretted it afterwards, I didn't let you down,
buddy! Thanks to the whole team at Ubisoft Montreal for their time and patience. Benjamin Dennel –
thank you, my friend, for the motivation and encouragement. And a huge thanks to François Tallec,
for supporting me during the creation of the album – I know it wasn't easy!

DEFALI

Thank you to Yves Guillemot, Alain Corre, Serge Hascoet, Jade Raymond, Patrice Desilets, Corey
May, Sébastien Puel, Mohamed Gambouz, Olivier Henriot, Mathieu Ferland, Audrey-Ann Milot,
Tommy Francois, Thomas Paincon, Florent Greffe and Marie-Anne Boutet.
Thanks also to Vladimir Lentzy, Philippe Hédouin, Frédéric Noaro and the rest of the team at
Dargaud for their support.

LES DEUX ROYAUMES

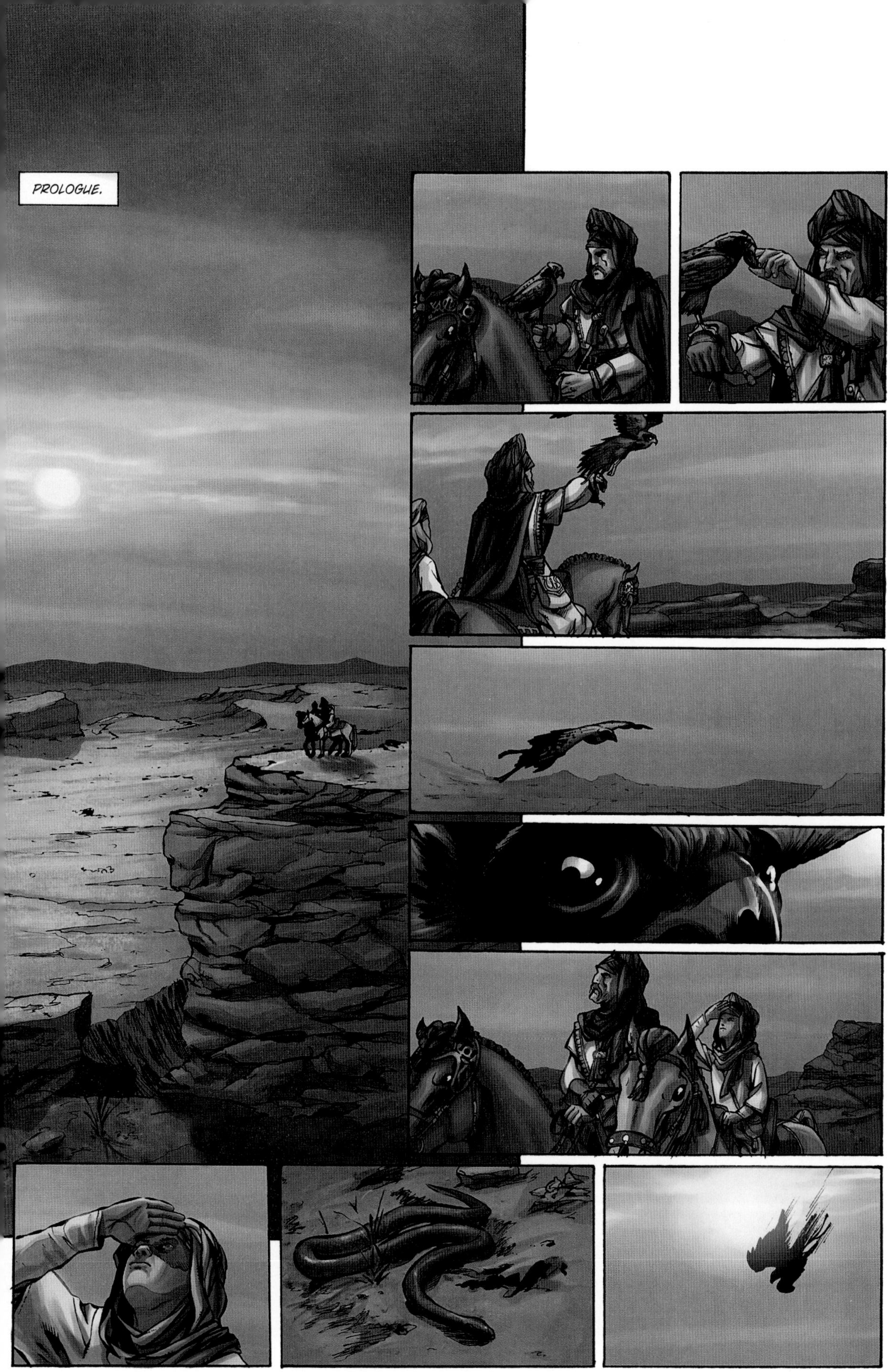
PROLOGUE.

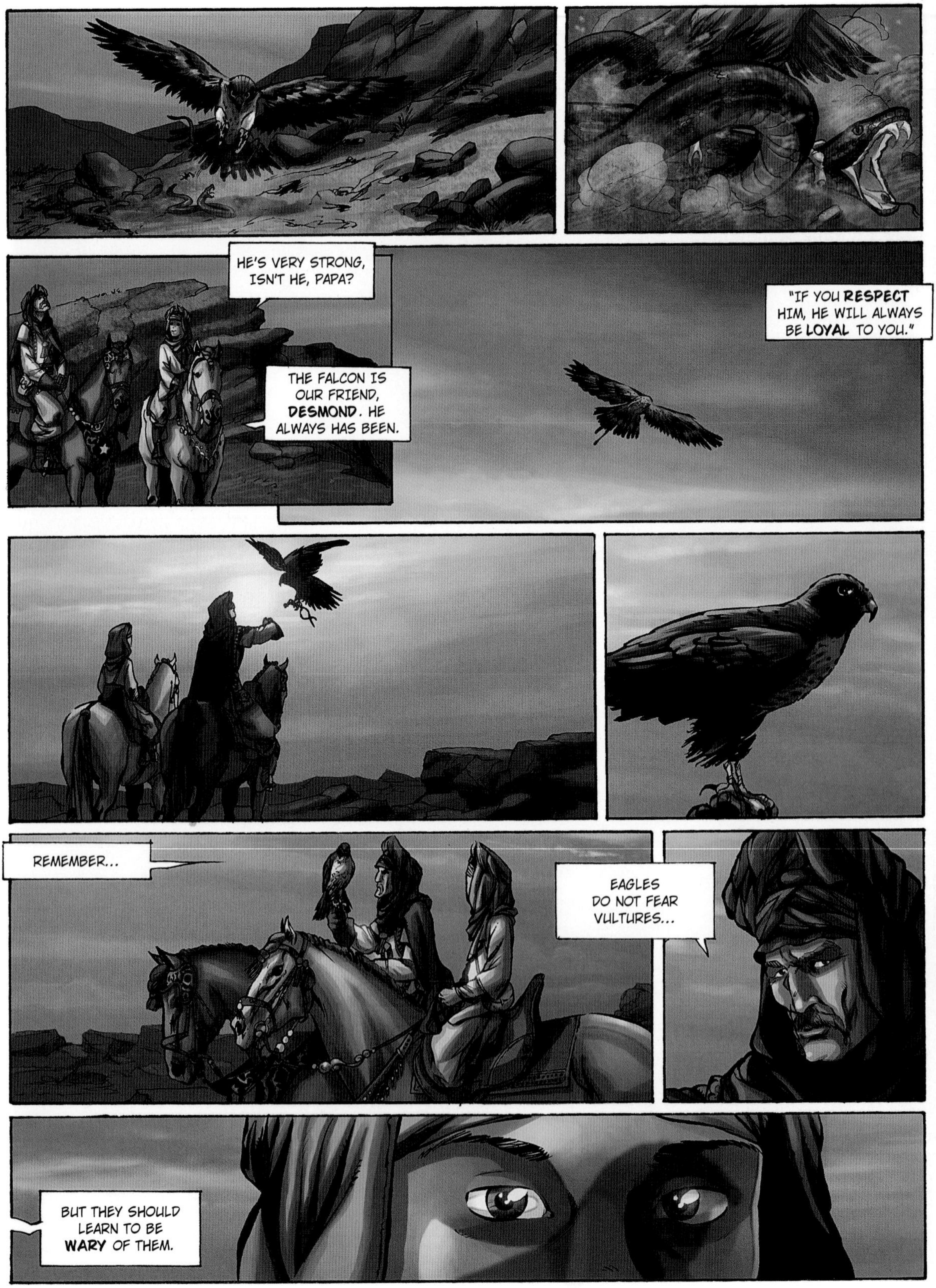

HE'S VERY STRONG, ISN'T HE, PAPA?
THE FALCON IS OUR FRIEND, DESMOND. HE ALWAYS HAS BEEN.
"IF YOU RESPECT HIM, HE WILL ALWAYS BE LOYAL TO YOU."
REMEMBER...
EAGLES DO NOT FEAR VULTURES...
BUT THEY SHOULD LEARN TO BE WARY OF THEM.

2

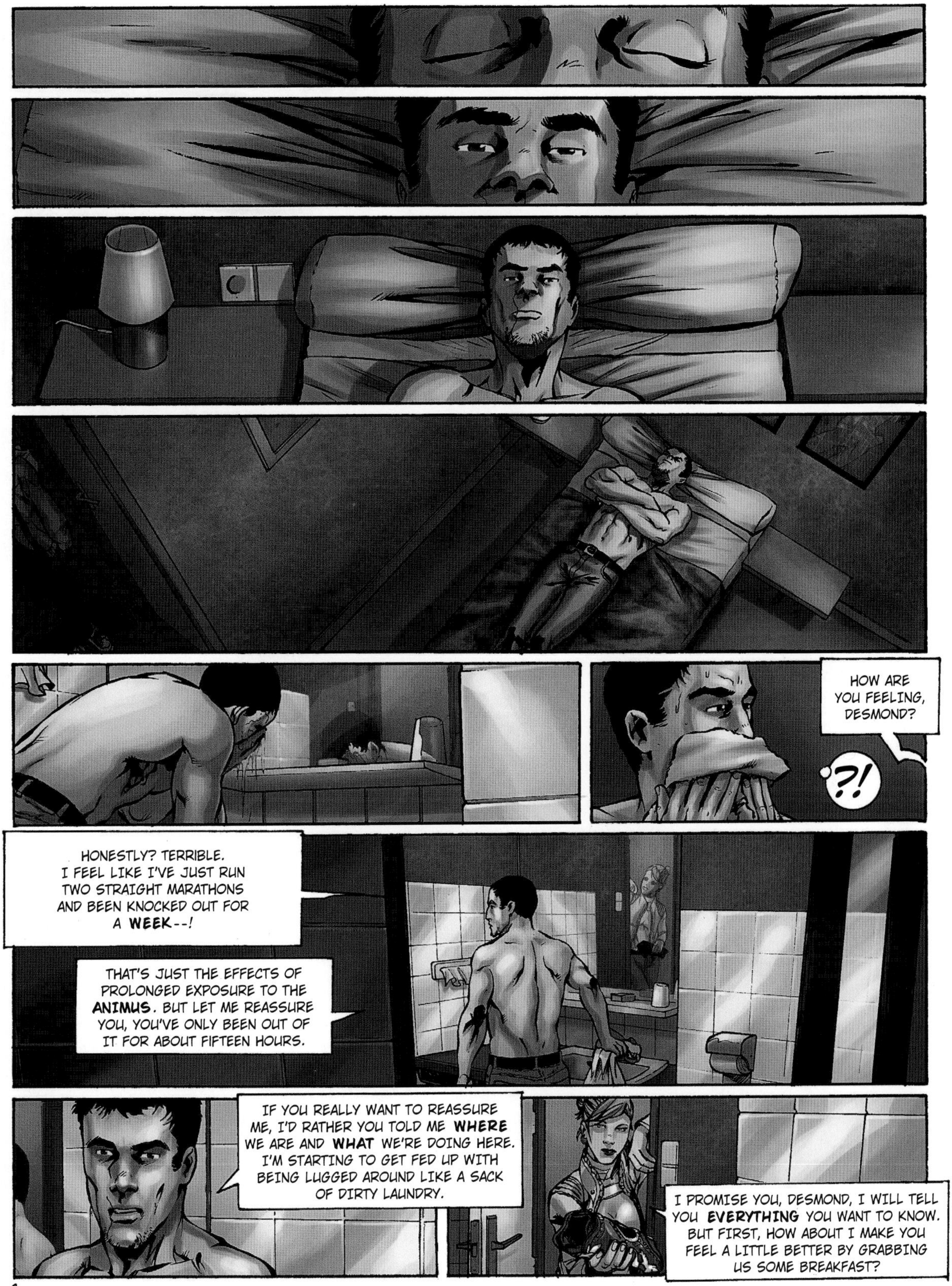
HOW ARE YOU FEELING, DESMOND?
?!
HONESTLY? TERRIBLE. I FEEL LIKE I'VE JUST RUN TWO STRAIGHT MARATHONS AND BEEN KNOCKED OUT FOR A **WEEK**--!
THAT'S JUST THE EFFECTS OF PROLONGED EXPOSURE TO THE **ANIMUS**. BUT LET ME REASSURE YOU, YOU'VE ONLY BEEN OUT OF IT FOR ABOUT FIFTEEN HOURS.
IF YOU REALLY WANT TO REASSURE ME, I'D RATHER YOU TOLD ME **WHERE** WE ARE AND **WHAT** WE'RE DOING HERE. I'M STARTING TO GET FED UP WITH BEING LUGGED AROUND LIKE A SACK OF DIRTY LAUNDRY.
I PROMISE YOU, DESMOND, I WILL TELL YOU **EVERYTHING** YOU WANT TO KNOW. BUT FIRST, HOW ABOUT I MAKE YOU FEEL A LITTLE BETTER BY GRABBING US SOME BREAKFAST?

"I CAN ONLY REMEMBER **BITS**...

"I REMEMBER ESCAPING **ABSTERGO** WITH YOU.

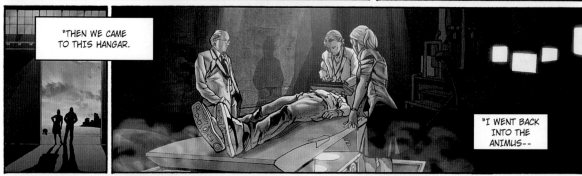

"THEN WE CAME TO THIS HANGAR.

"I WENT BACK INTO THE ANIMUS--

THERE HAVE BEEN SOME OTHER **DEVELOPMENTS** SINCE YOU RE-ENTERED THE ANIMUS. CLAY ESCAPED SOON AFTER REGAINING CONSCIOUSNESS AND TOM HAS BEEN SENT ON ANOTHER MISSION-

I ALSO REMEMBER SOME OTHER CONFUSING BITS AND PIECES. I WAS IN VENICE AND FLORENCE... IT WAS EVENTFUL AND BLOODY, TO SAY THE **LEAST**.

"AND THEN I WOKE UP HERE, IN THIS BEDROOM."

THERE ARE IMAGES FROM MY PAST CONTINUOUSLY **FLASHING** ACROSS MY MIND. WHY CAN'T I **FOCUS** ON THEM?

WE'VE GOT ALL THE DATA FROM **THAT** ADVENTURE, DESMOND. YOUR ANCESTOR, **EZIO**, HAS BEEN VERY USEFUL TO US.

AS EZIO OR ANY OF YOUR OTHER ANCESTRAL SUBJECTS, YOU ARE UNABLE TO RETAIN **ALL** THE INFORMATION IN YOUR MEMORY--WHICH IS PRETTY LUCKY, BECAUSE THERE'S JUST TOO MUCH OF IT! ON THE PLUS SIDE, YOUR TIME SPENT IN THE ANIMUS AS YOUR ANCESTORS IS BEGINNING TO **PENETRATE** YOUR MIND ON A **SUBCONSCIOUS LEVEL** IN THE PRESENT DAY.

4

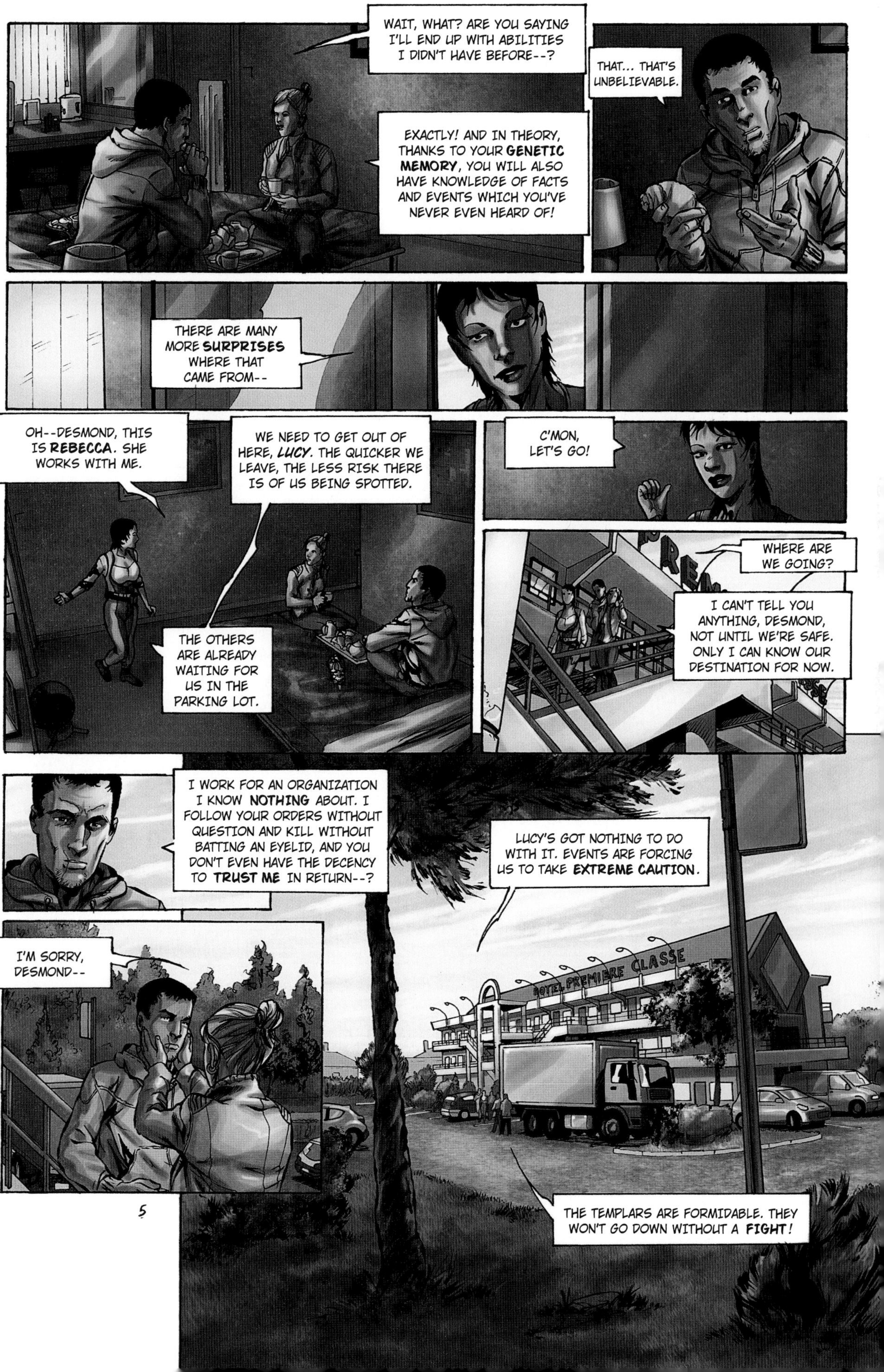

WAIT, WHAT? ARE YOU SAYING I'LL END UP WITH ABILITIES I DIDN'T HAVE BEFORE--?
EXACTLY! AND IN THEORY, THANKS TO YOUR GENETIC MEMORY, YOU WILL ALSO HAVE KNOWLEDGE OF FACTS AND EVENTS WHICH YOU'VE NEVER EVEN HEARD OF!
THAT... THAT'S UNBELIEVABLE.
THERE ARE MANY MORE SURPRISES WHERE THAT CAME FROM--
OH--DESMOND, THIS IS REBECCA. SHE WORKS WITH ME.
WE NEED TO GET OUT OF HERE, LUCY. THE QUICKER WE LEAVE, THE LESS RISK THERE IS OF US BEING SPOTTED.
THE OTHERS ARE ALREADY WAITING FOR US IN THE PARKING LOT.
C'MON, LET'S GO!
WHERE ARE WE GOING?
I CAN'T TELL YOU ANYTHING, DESMOND, NOT UNTIL WE'RE SAFE. ONLY I CAN KNOW OUR DESTINATION FOR NOW.
I WORK FOR AN ORGANIZATION I KNOW NOTHING ABOUT. I FOLLOW YOUR ORDERS WITHOUT QUESTION AND KILL WITHOUT BATTING AN EYELID, AND YOU DON'T EVEN HAVE THE DECENCY TO TRUST ME IN RETURN--?
LUCY'S GOT NOTHING TO DO WITH IT. EVENTS ARE FORCING US TO TAKE EXTREME CAUTION.
I'M SORRY, DESMOND--
HOTEL PREMIERE CLASSE
THE TEMPLARS ARE FORMIDABLE. THEY WON'T GO DOWN WITHOUT A FIGHT!

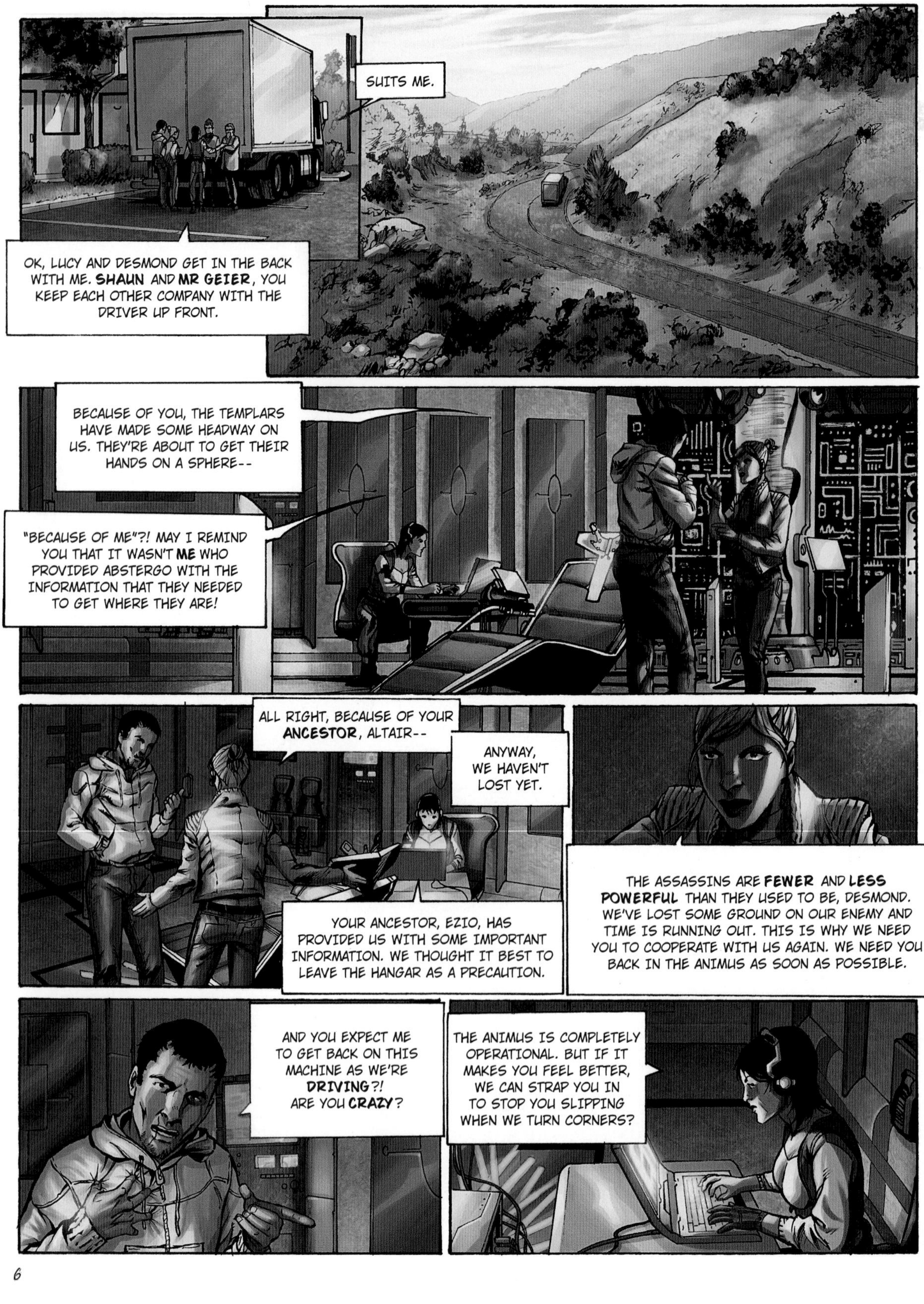
SUITS ME.
OK, LUCY AND DESMOND GET IN THE BACK WITH ME. SHAUN AND MR GEIER, YOU KEEP EACH OTHER COMPANY WITH THE DRIVER UP FRONT.
BECAUSE OF YOU, THE TEMPLARS HAVE MADE SOME HEADWAY ON US. THEY'RE ABOUT TO GET THEIR HANDS ON A SPHERE--
"BECAUSE OF ME"?! MAY I REMIND YOU THAT IT WASN'T ME WHO PROVIDED ABSTERGO WITH THE INFORMATION THAT THEY NEEDED TO GET WHERE THEY ARE!
ALL RIGHT, BECAUSE OF YOUR ANCESTOR, ALTAIR--
ANYWAY, WE HAVEN'T LOST YET.
YOUR ANCESTOR, EZIO, HAS PROVIDED US WITH SOME IMPORTANT INFORMATION. WE THOUGHT IT BEST TO LEAVE THE HANGAR AS A PRECAUTION.
THE ASSASSINS ARE FEWER AND LESS POWERFUL THAN THEY USED TO BE, DESMOND. WE'VE LOST SOME GROUND ON OUR ENEMY AND TIME IS RUNNING OUT. THIS IS WHY WE NEED YOU TO COOPERATE WITH US AGAIN. WE NEED YOU BACK IN THE ANIMUS AS SOON AS POSSIBLE.
AND YOU EXPECT ME TO GET BACK ON THIS MACHINE AS WE'RE DRIVING?! ARE YOU CRAZY?
THE ANIMUS IS COMPLETELY OPERATIONAL. BUT IF IT MAKES YOU FEEL BETTER, WE CAN STRAP YOU IN TO STOP YOU SLIPPING WHEN WE TURN CORNERS?
6

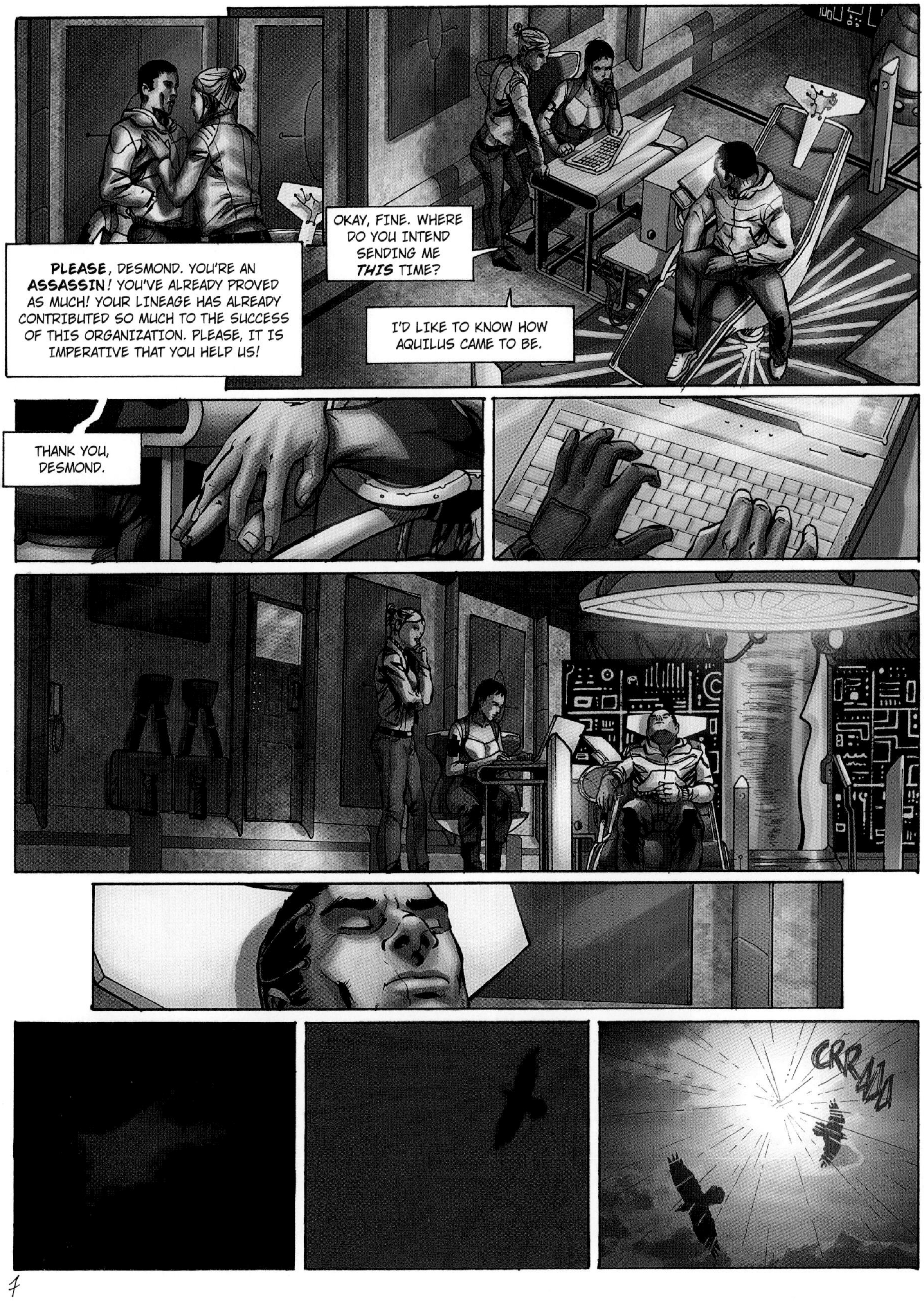
PLEASE, DESMOND. YOU'RE AN ASSASSIN! YOU'VE ALREADY PROVED AS MUCH! YOUR LINEAGE HAS ALREADY CONTRIBUTED SO MUCH TO THE SUCCESS OF THIS ORGANIZATION. PLEASE, IT IS IMPERATIVE THAT YOU HELP US!
OKAY, FINE. WHERE DO YOU INTEND SENDING ME THIS TIME?
I'D LIKE TO KNOW HOW AQUILUS CAME TO BE.
THANK YOU, DESMOND.
CRRAAA

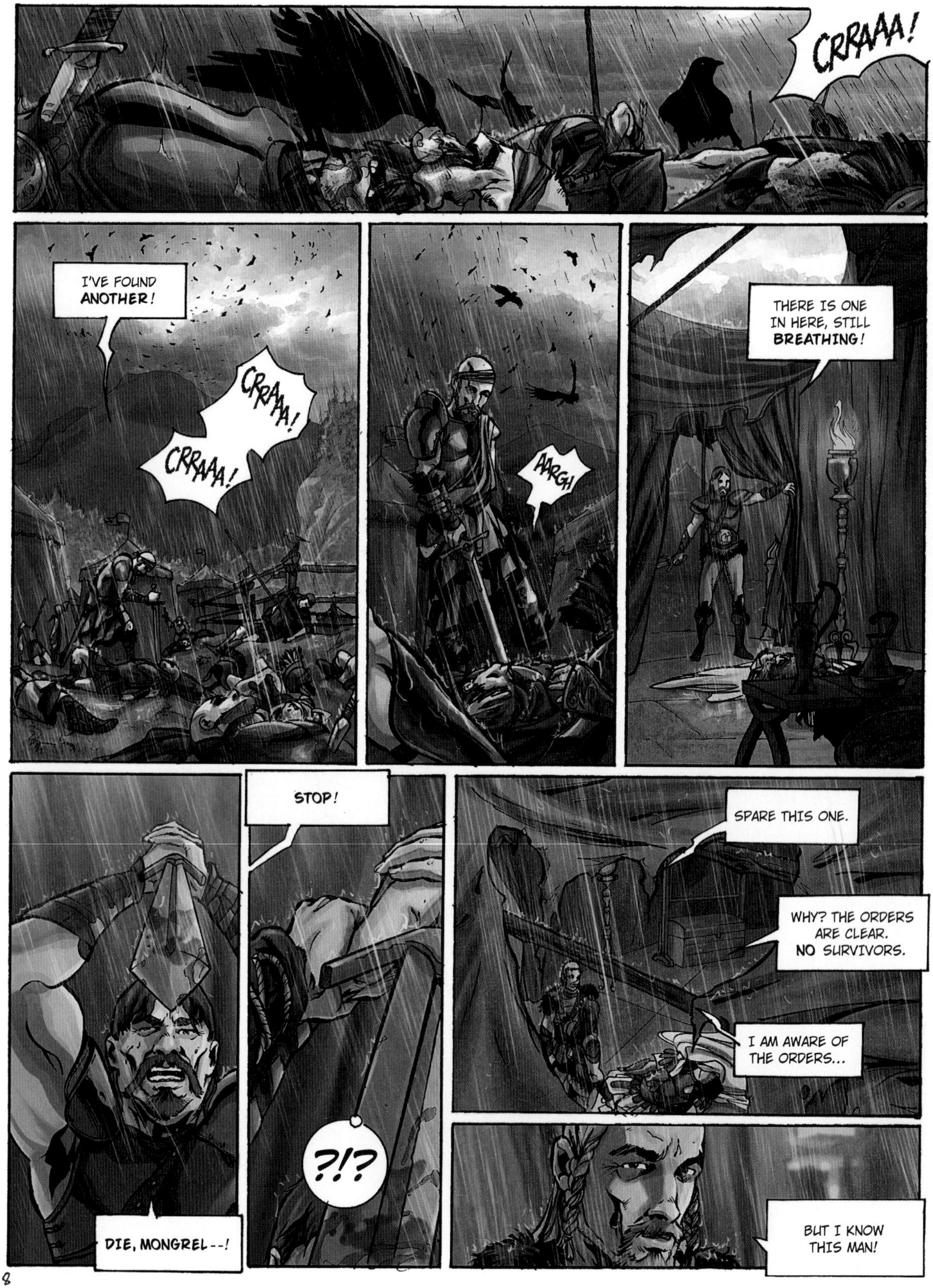
CRRAAA!
I'VE FOUND ANOTHER!
CRRAAA!
CRRAAA!
AARGH
THERE IS ONE IN HERE, STILL BREATHING!
DIE, MONGREL--!
STOP!
?!?
SPARE THIS ONE.
WHY? THE ORDERS ARE CLEAR. NO SURVIVORS.
I AM AWARE OF THE ORDERS...
BUT I KNOW THIS MAN!
8

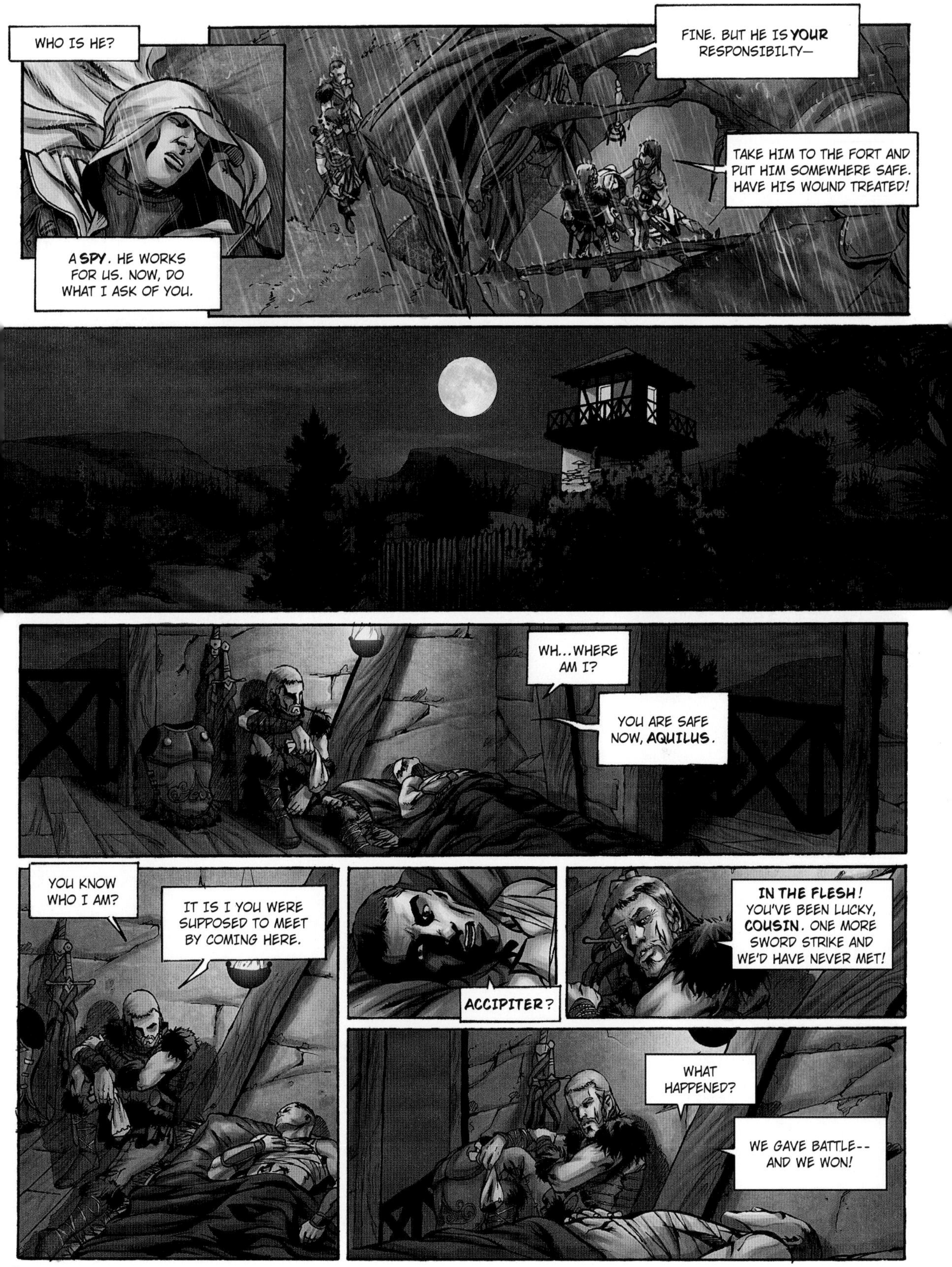
WHO IS HE?
A SPY. HE WORKS FOR US. NOW, DO WHAT I ASK OF YOU.
FINE. BUT HE IS YOUR RESPONSIBILTY—
TAKE HIM TO THE FORT AND PUT HIM SOMEWHERE SAFE. HAVE HIS WOUND TREATED!
WH...WHERE AM I?
YOU ARE SAFE NOW, AQUILUS.
YOU KNOW WHO I AM?
IT IS I YOU WERE SUPPOSED TO MEET BY COMING HERE.
ACCIPITER?
IN THE FLESH! YOU'VE BEEN LUCKY, COUSIN. ONE MORE SWORD STRIKE AND WE'D HAVE NEVER MET!
WHAT HAPPENED?
WE GAVE BATTLE-- AND WE WON!
9

"FOR MANY MONTHS, OUR TROOPS CROSSED THE DANUBE AND THE RHINE. WE ATTEMPTED TO MARCH OVER THE ROMAN BORDERS BY ATTACKING THE ENEMY CAMPS AND FORTIFICATIONS.

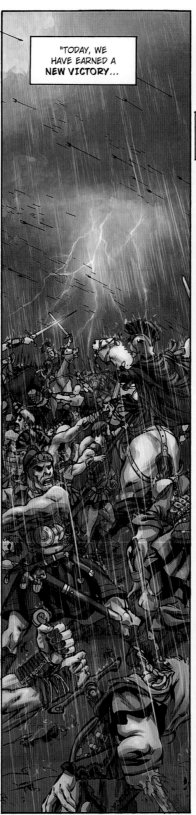

"TODAY, WE HAVE EARNED A **NEW VICTORY**...

"THE ROUTE TO THE WEST WILL SOON OPEN ITSELF BEFORE US!"

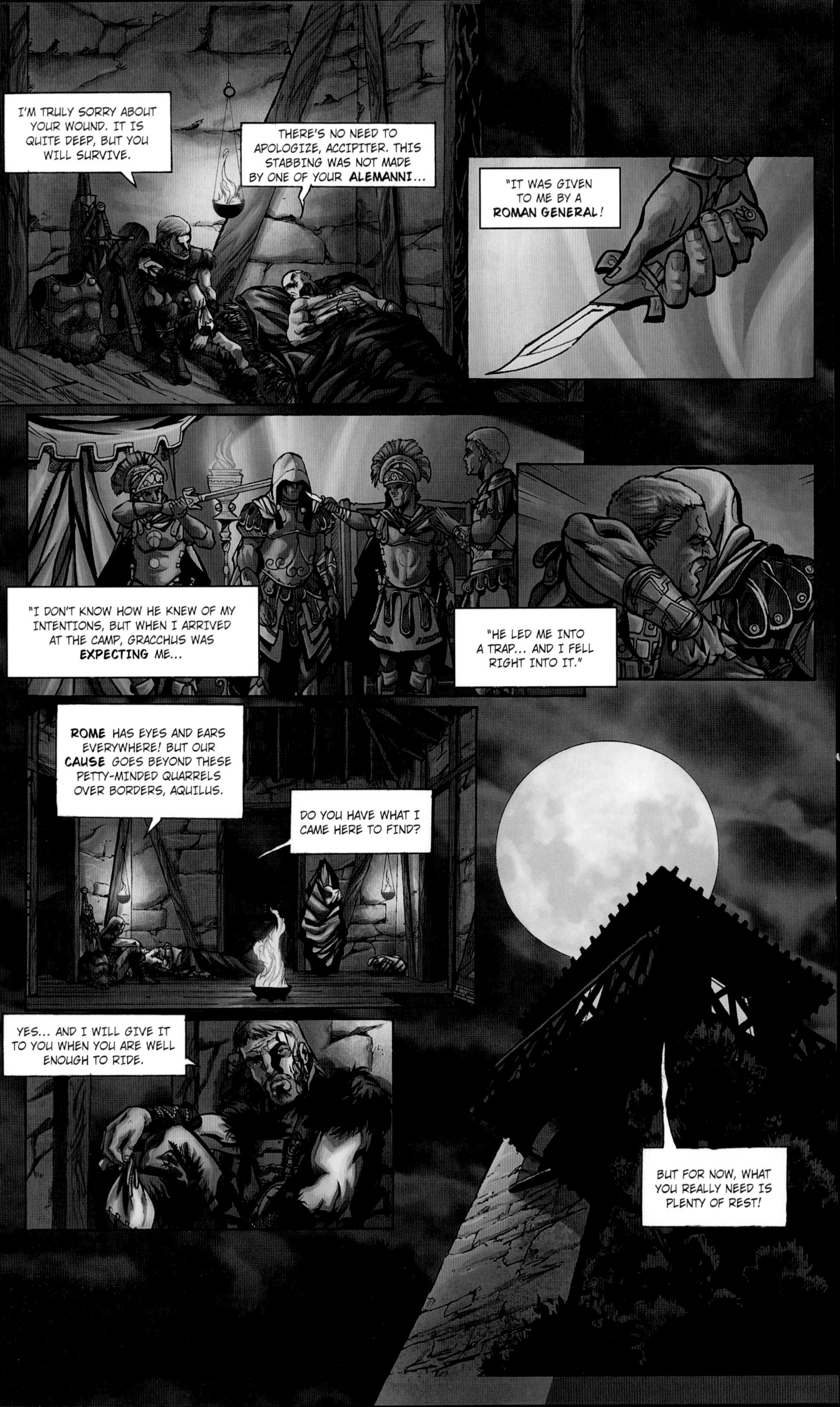
I'M TRULY SORRY ABOUT YOUR WOUND. IT IS QUITE DEEP, BUT YOU WILL SURVIVE.
THERE'S NO NEED TO APOLOGIZE, ACCIPITER. THIS STABBING WAS NOT MADE BY ONE OF YOUR **ALEMANNI**...
"IT WAS GIVEN TO ME BY A **ROMAN GENERAL**!
"I DON'T KNOW HOW HE KNEW OF MY INTENTIONS, BUT WHEN I ARRIVED AT THE CAMP, GRACCHUS WAS **EXPECTING** ME...
"HE LED ME INTO A TRAP... AND I FELL RIGHT INTO IT."
ROME HAS EYES AND EARS EVERYWHERE! BUT OUR **CAUSE** GOES BEYOND THESE PETTY-MINDED QUARRELS OVER BORDERS, AQUILUS.
DO YOU HAVE WHAT I CAME HERE TO FIND?
YES... AND I WILL GIVE IT TO YOU WHEN YOU ARE WELL ENOUGH TO RIDE.
BUT FOR NOW, WHAT YOU REALLY NEED IS PLENTY OF REST!

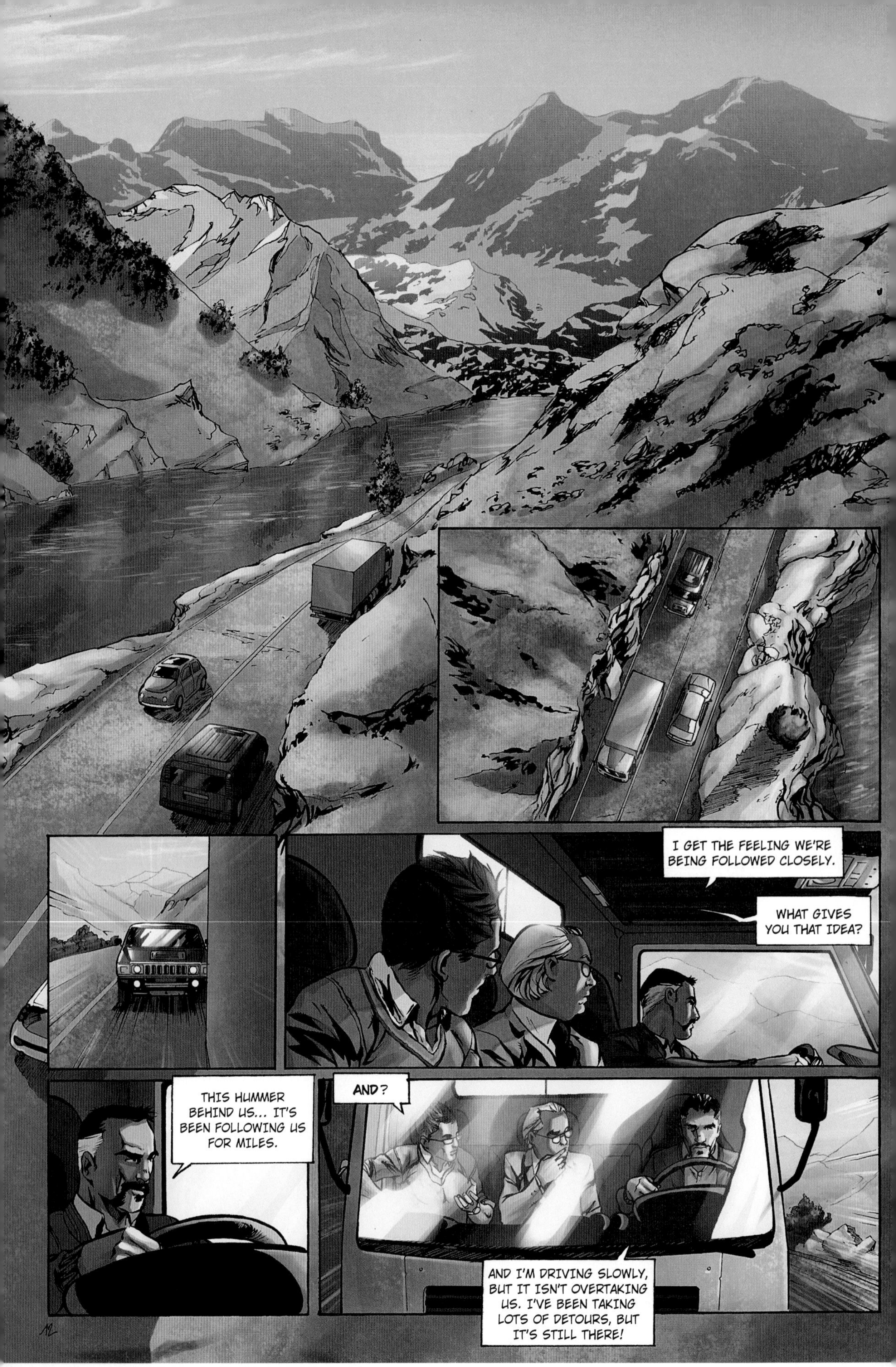
I GET THE FEELING WE'RE BEING FOLLOWED CLOSELY.
WHAT GIVES YOU THAT IDEA?
THIS HUMMER BEHIND US... IT'S BEEN FOLLOWING US FOR MILES.
AND?
AND I'M DRIVING SLOWLY, BUT IT ISN'T OVERTAKING US. I'VE BEEN TAKING LOTS OF DETOURS, BUT IT'S STILL THERE!

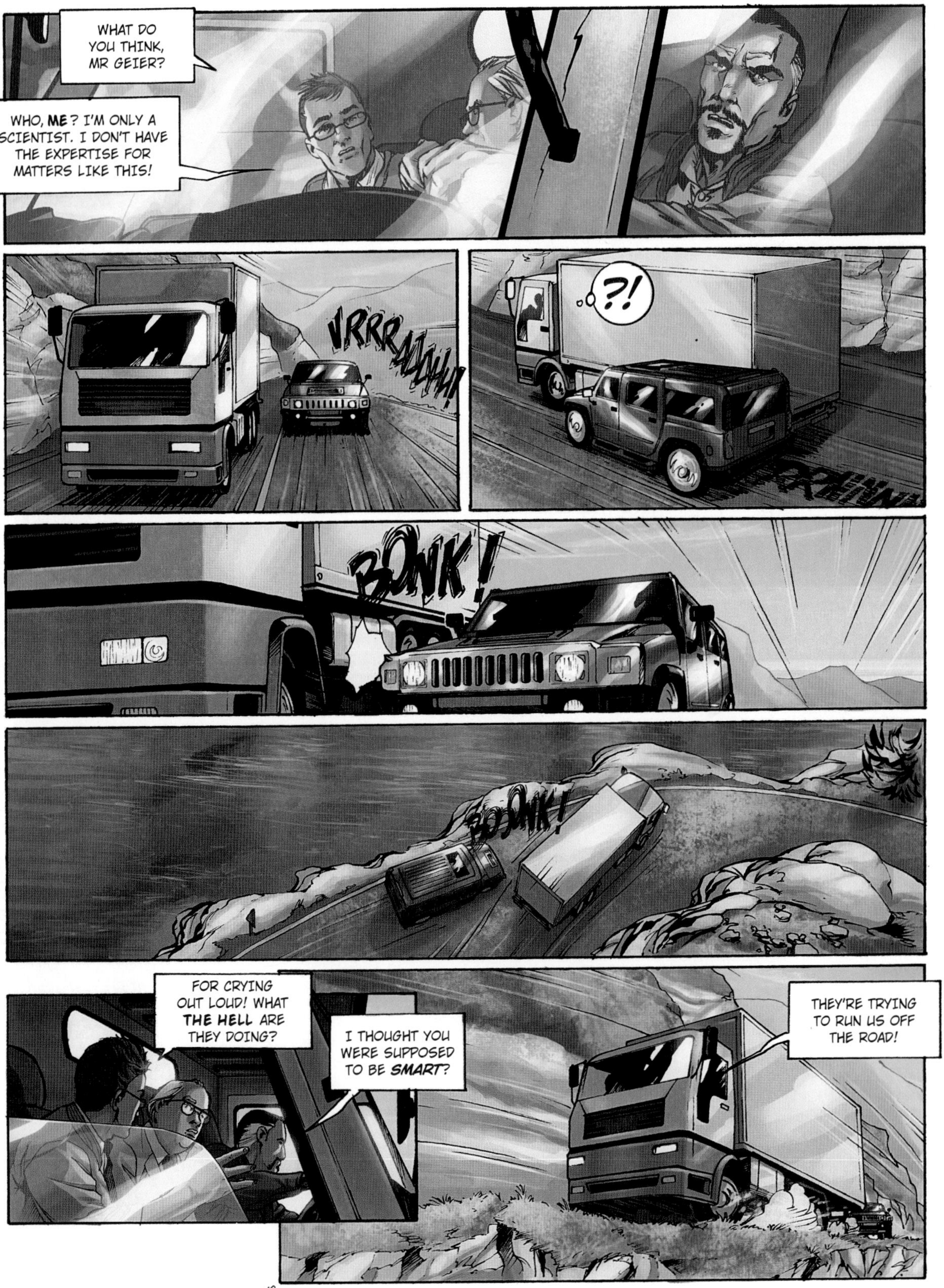
WHAT DO YOU THINK, MR GEIER?
WHO, ME? I'M ONLY A SCIENTIST. I DON'T HAVE THE EXPERTISE FOR MATTERS LIKE THIS!
?!
BONK!
FOR CRYING OUT LOUD! WHAT THE HELL ARE THEY DOING?
I THOUGHT YOU WERE SUPPOSED TO BE SMART?
THEY'RE TRYING TO RUN US OFF THE ROAD!

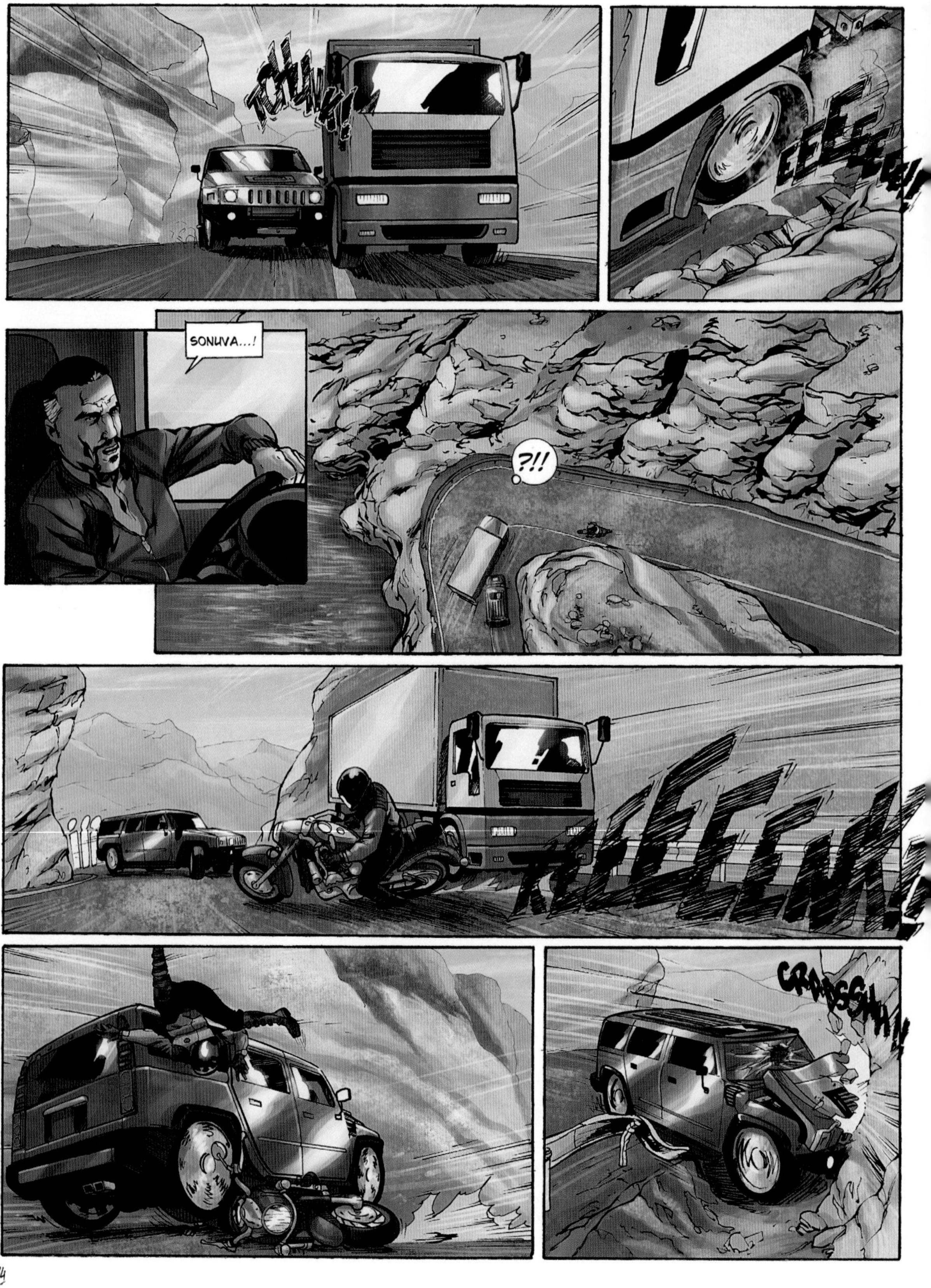
TCHUNK!!
SONUVA...!
?!!
CRAASSGHH!!

14

ATTACKED*!?!*

WE WERE BEING ATTACKED—

UHH--YES.

YES, LUCY?

TELL ME WHAT JUST HAPPENED, **HERMAN**?

BUT DON'T WORRY, THE DANGER DEFINITELY SEEMS TO HAVE BEEN REMOVED.

ARE YOU SURE?

ABSOLUTELY.

HOW'S DESMOND?

NO DISRUPTION. THE SESSION IS CONTINUING AS NORMAL.

15

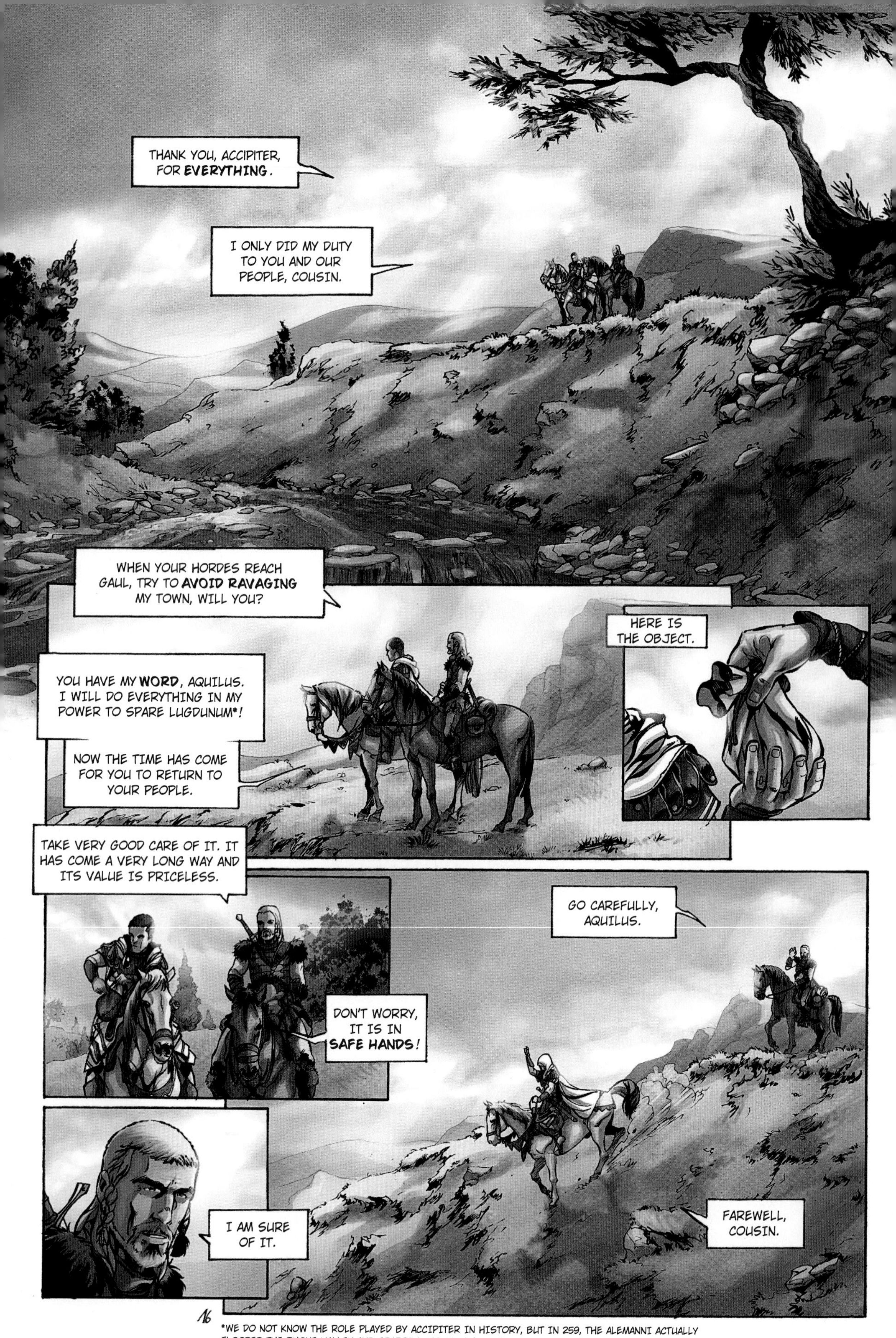
THANK YOU, ACCIPITER, FOR EVERYTHING.
I ONLY DID MY DUTY TO YOU AND OUR PEOPLE, COUSIN.
WHEN YOUR HORDES REACH GAUL, TRY TO AVOID RAVAGING MY TOWN, WILL YOU?
YOU HAVE MY WORD, AQUILUS. I WILL DO EVERYTHING IN MY POWER TO SPARE LUGDUNUM*!
NOW THE TIME HAS COME FOR YOU TO RETURN TO YOUR PEOPLE.
HERE IS THE OBJECT.
TAKE VERY GOOD CARE OF IT. IT HAS COME A VERY LONG WAY AND ITS VALUE IS PRICELESS.
DON'T WORRY, IT IS IN SAFE HANDS!
I AM SURE OF IT.
GO CAREFULLY, AQUILUS.
FAREWELL, COUSIN.
16

*WE DO NOT KNOW THE ROLE PLAYED BY ACCIPITER IN HISTORY, BUT IN 259, THE ALEMANNI ACTUALLY FLOODED THE RHONE VALLEY AND SPARED LUGDUNUM (KNOWN TODAY AS THE TOWN OF LYON).

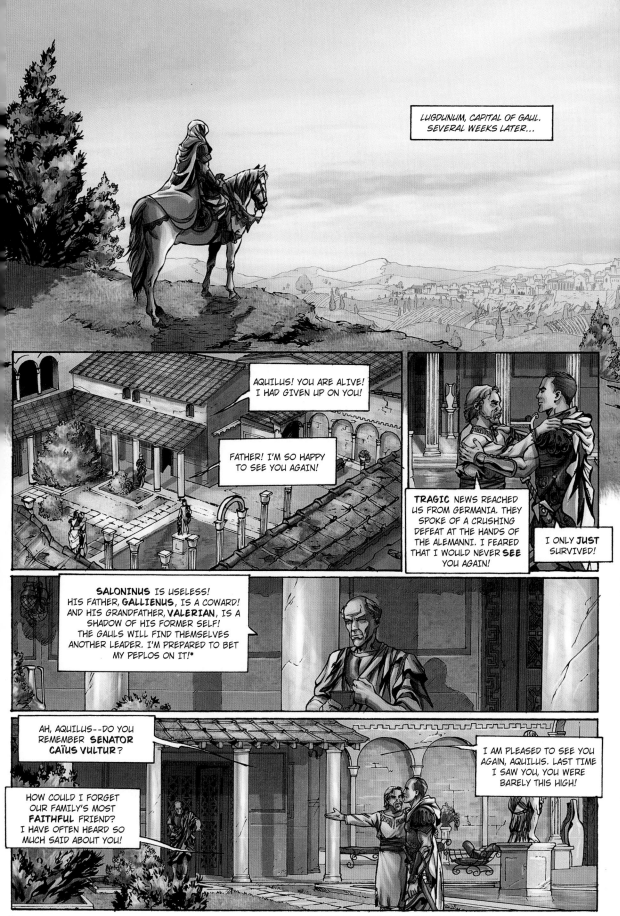

LUGDUNUM, CAPITAL OF GAUL. SEVERAL WEEKS LATER...

AQUILUS! YOU ARE ALIVE! I HAD GIVEN UP ON YOU!

FATHER! I'M SO HAPPY TO SEE YOU AGAIN!

TRAGIC NEWS REACHED US FROM GERMANIA. THEY SPOKE OF A CRUSHING DEFEAT AT THE HANDS OF THE ALEMANNI. I FEARED THAT I WOULD NEVER SEE YOU AGAIN!

I ONLY JUST SURVIVED!

SALONINUS IS USELESS! HIS FATHER, GALLIENUS, IS A COWARD! AND HIS GRANDFATHER, VALERIAN, IS A SHADOW OF HIS FORMER SELF! THE GAULS WILL FIND THEMSELVES ANOTHER LEADER. I'M PREPARED TO BET MY PEPLOS ON IT!*

AH, AQUILUS--DO YOU REMEMBER SENATOR CAÏUS VULTUR?

I AM PLEASED TO SEE YOU AGAIN, AQUILUS. LAST TIME I SAW YOU, YOU WERE BARELY THIS HIGH!

HOW COULD I FORGET OUR FAMILY'S MOST FAITHFUL FRIEND? I HAVE OFTEN HEARD SO MUCH SAID ABOUT YOU!

17

*SALONINUS, GALLIENUS, AND VALERIAN SHARED POWER AND RULED THE ROMAN EMPIRE.

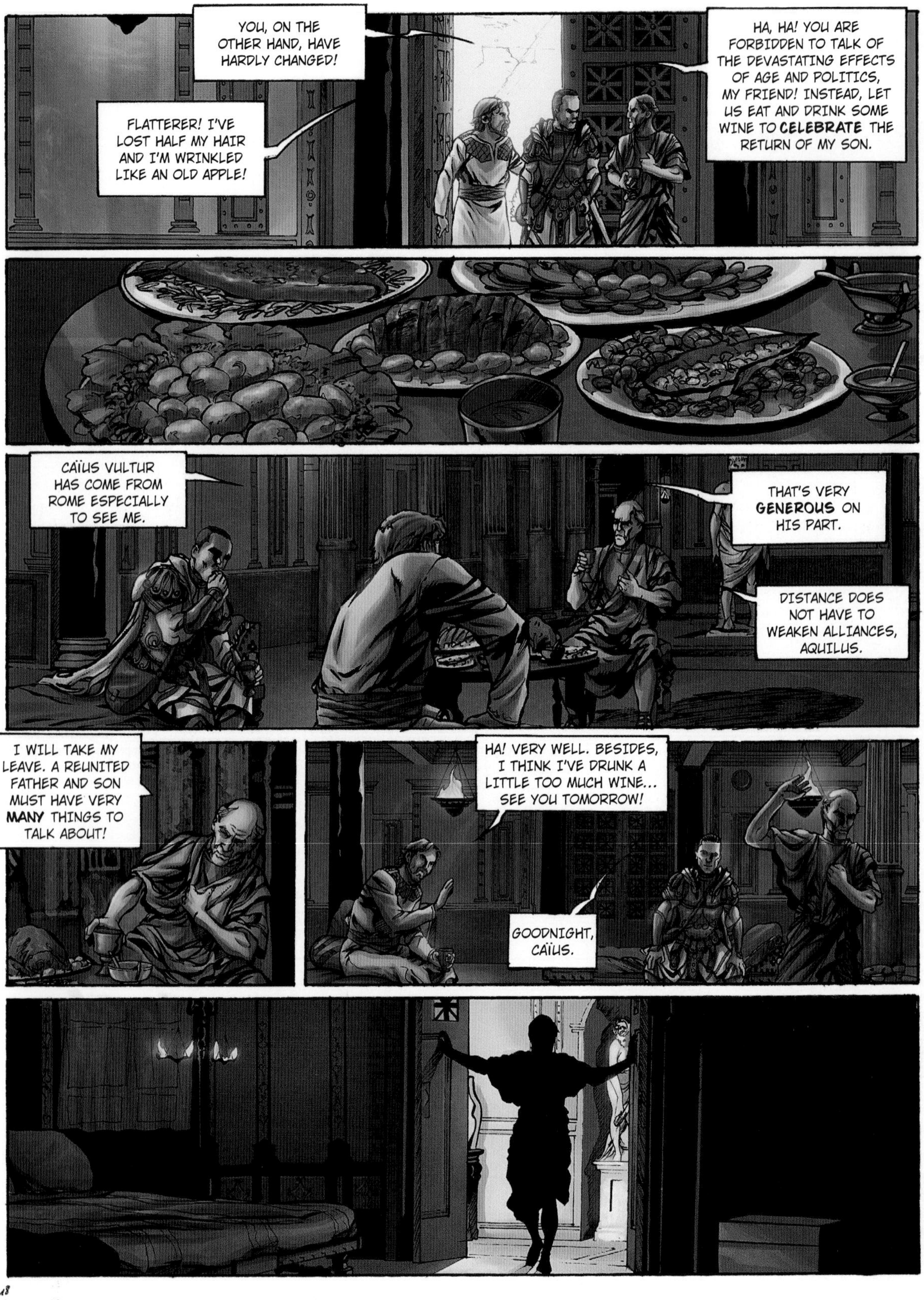
YOU, ON THE OTHER HAND, HAVE HARDLY CHANGED!
FLATTERER! I'VE LOST HALF MY HAIR AND I'M WRINKLED LIKE AN OLD APPLE!
HA, HA! YOU ARE FORBIDDEN TO TALK OF THE DEVASTATING EFFECTS OF AGE AND POLITICS, MY FRIEND! INSTEAD, LET US EAT AND DRINK SOME WINE TO **CELEBRATE** THE RETURN OF MY SON.
CAÏUS VULTUR HAS COME FROM ROME ESPECIALLY TO SEE ME.
THAT'S VERY **GENEROUS** ON HIS PART.
DISTANCE DOES NOT HAVE TO WEAKEN ALLIANCES, AQUILUS.
I WILL TAKE MY LEAVE. A REUNITED FATHER AND SON MUST HAVE VERY **MANY** THINGS TO TALK ABOUT!
HA! VERY WELL. BESIDES, I THINK I'VE DRUNK A LITTLE TOO MUCH WINE... SEE YOU TOMORROW!
GOODNIGHT, CAÏUS.
18

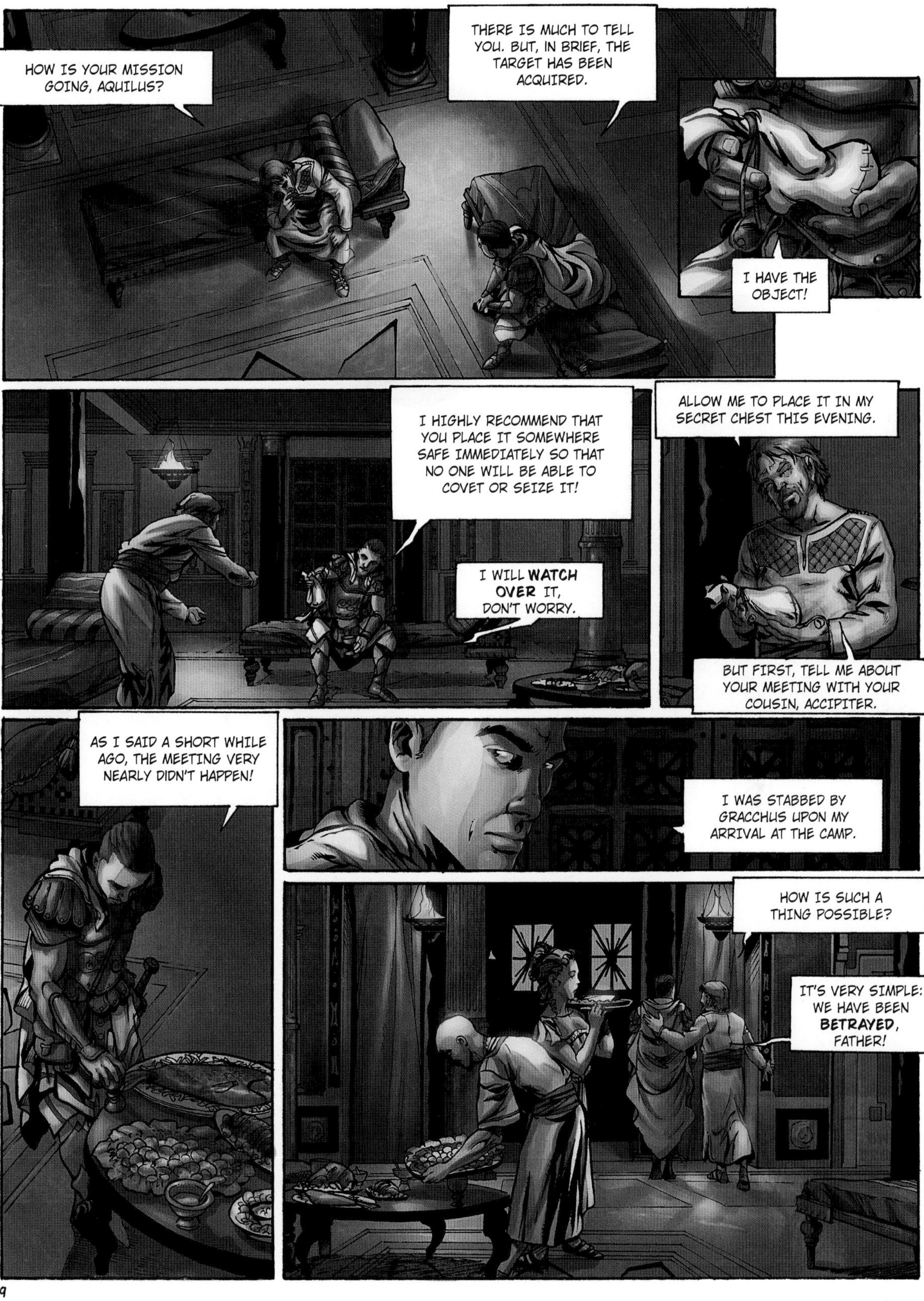
HOW IS YOUR MISSION GOING, AQUILUS?
THERE IS MUCH TO TELL YOU. BUT, IN BRIEF, THE TARGET HAS BEEN ACQUIRED.
I HAVE THE OBJECT!
I HIGHLY RECOMMEND THAT YOU PLACE IT SOMEWHERE SAFE IMMEDIATELY SO THAT NO ONE WILL BE ABLE TO COVET OR SEIZE IT!
I WILL **WATCH OVER** IT, DON'T WORRY.
ALLOW ME TO PLACE IT IN MY SECRET CHEST THIS EVENING.
BUT FIRST, TELL ME ABOUT YOUR MEETING WITH YOUR COUSIN, ACCIPITER.
AS I SAID A SHORT WHILE AGO, THE MEETING VERY NEARLY DIDN'T HAPPEN!
I WAS STABBED BY GRACCHUS UPON MY ARRIVAL AT THE CAMP.
HOW IS SUCH A THING POSSIBLE?
IT'S VERY SIMPLE: WE HAVE BEEN **BETRAYED**, FATHER!

19

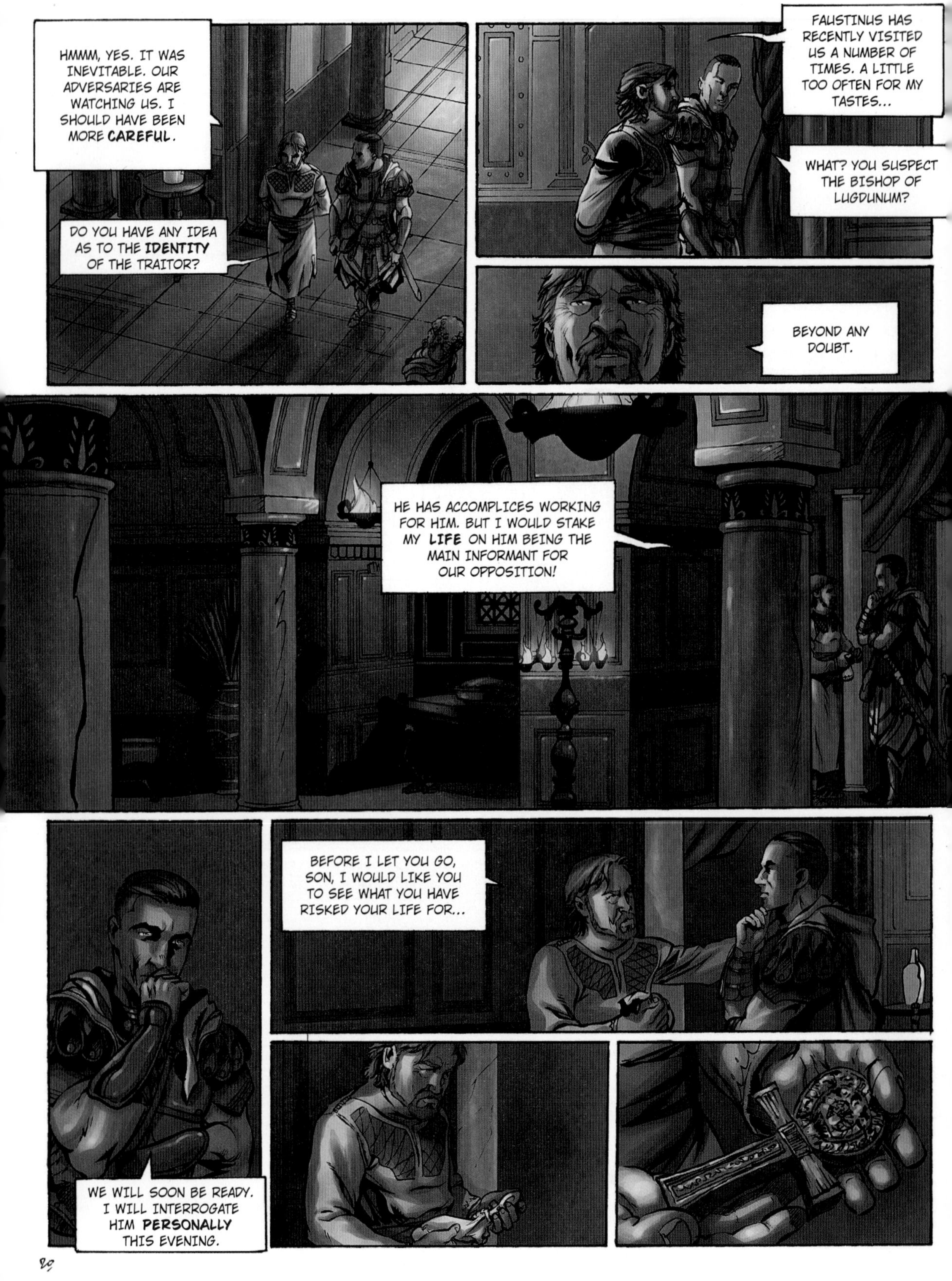
HMMM, YES. IT WAS INEVITABLE. OUR ADVERSARIES ARE WATCHING US. I SHOULD HAVE BEEN MORE CAREFUL.
DO YOU HAVE ANY IDEA AS TO THE IDENTITY OF THE TRAITOR?
FAUSTINUS HAS RECENTLY VISITED US A NUMBER OF TIMES. A LITTLE TOO OFTEN FOR MY TASTES...
WHAT? YOU SUSPECT THE BISHOP OF LUGDUNUM?
BEYOND ANY DOUBT.
HE HAS ACCOMPLICES WORKING FOR HIM. BUT I WOULD STAKE MY LIFE ON HIM BEING THE MAIN INFORMANT FOR OUR OPPOSITION!
WE WILL SOON BE READY. I WILL INTERROGATE HIM PERSONALLY THIS EVENING.
BEFORE I LET YOU GO, SON, I WOULD LIKE YOU TO SEE WHAT YOU HAVE RISKED YOUR LIFE FOR...

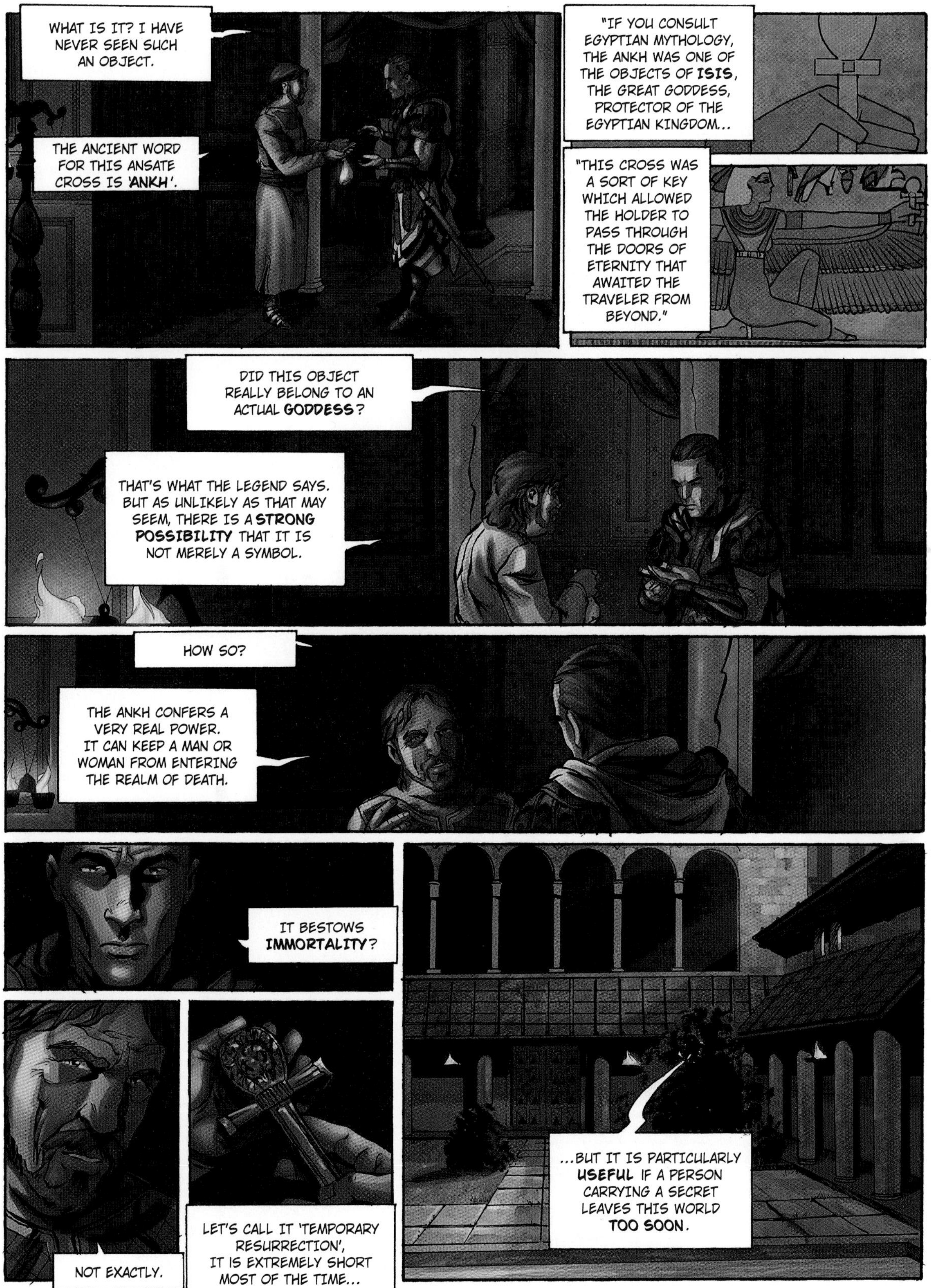
WHAT IS IT? I HAVE NEVER SEEN SUCH AN OBJECT.
THE ANCIENT WORD FOR THIS ANSATE CROSS IS 'ANKH'.
"IF YOU CONSULT EGYPTIAN MYTHOLOGY, THE ANKH WAS ONE OF THE OBJECTS OF ISIS, THE GREAT GODDESS, PROTECTOR OF THE EGYPTIAN KINGDOM...
"THIS CROSS WAS A SORT OF KEY WHICH ALLOWED THE HOLDER TO PASS THROUGH THE DOORS OF ETERNITY THAT AWAITED THE TRAVELER FROM BEYOND."
DID THIS OBJECT REALLY BELONG TO AN ACTUAL GODDESS?
THAT'S WHAT THE LEGEND SAYS. BUT AS UNLIKELY AS THAT MAY SEEM, THERE IS A STRONG POSSIBILITY THAT IT IS NOT MERELY A SYMBOL.
HOW SO?
THE ANKH CONFERS A VERY REAL POWER. IT CAN KEEP A MAN OR WOMAN FROM ENTERING THE REALM OF DEATH.
IT BESTOWS IMMORTALITY?
NOT EXACTLY.
LET'S CALL IT 'TEMPORARY RESURRECTION', IT IS EXTREMELY SHORT MOST OF THE TIME...
...BUT IT IS PARTICULARLY USEFUL IF A PERSON CARRYING A SECRET LEAVES THIS WORLD TOO SOON.
21

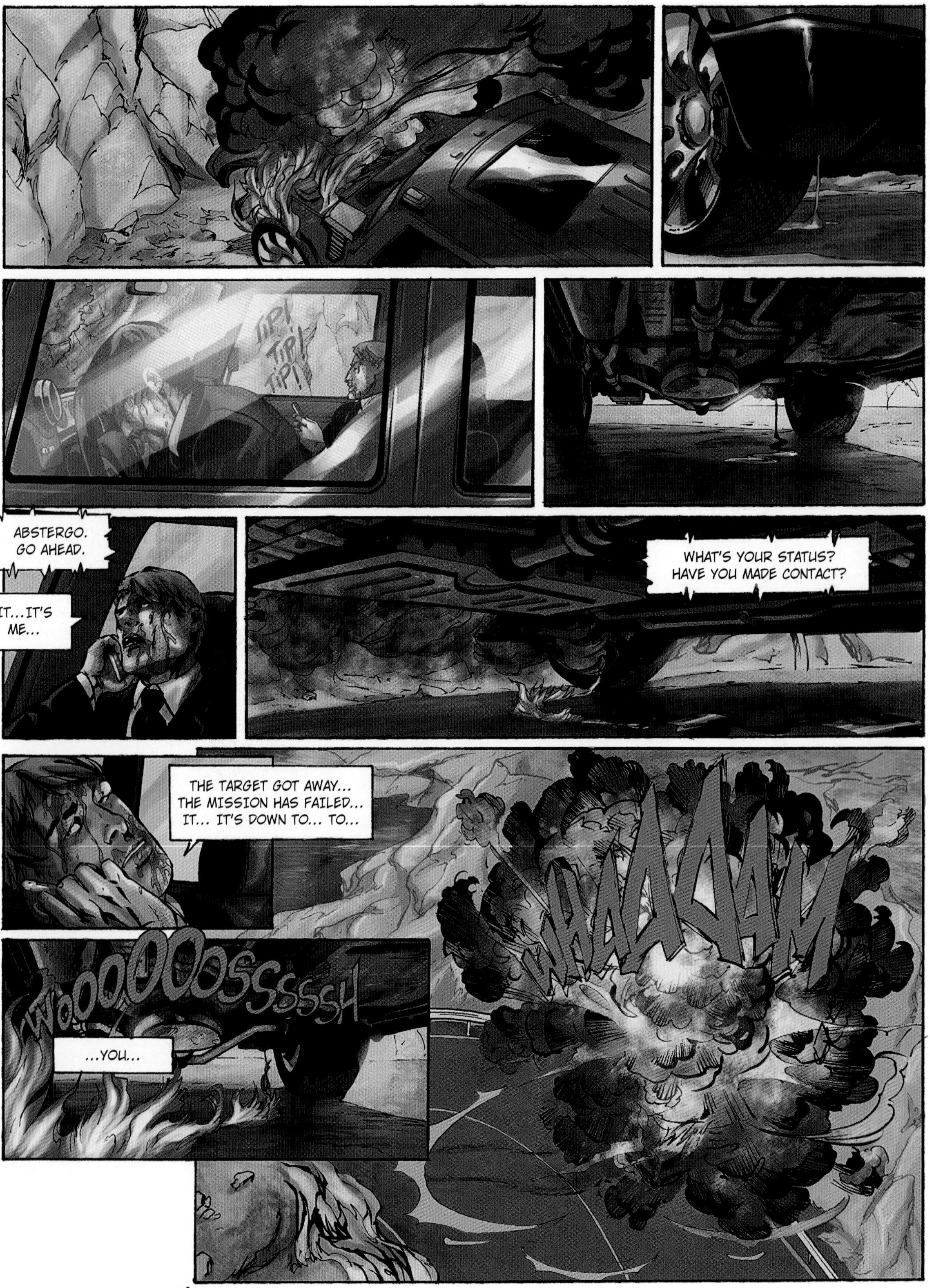
TIP!
TIP!
TIP!
ABSTERGO. GO AHEAD.
IT...IT'S ME...
WHAT'S YOUR STATUS? HAVE YOU MADE CONTACT?
THE TARGET GOT AWAY... THE MISSION HAS FAILED... IT... IT'S DOWN TO... TO...
WOOOOOOSSSSSH
...YOU...
WHAAAAM

22

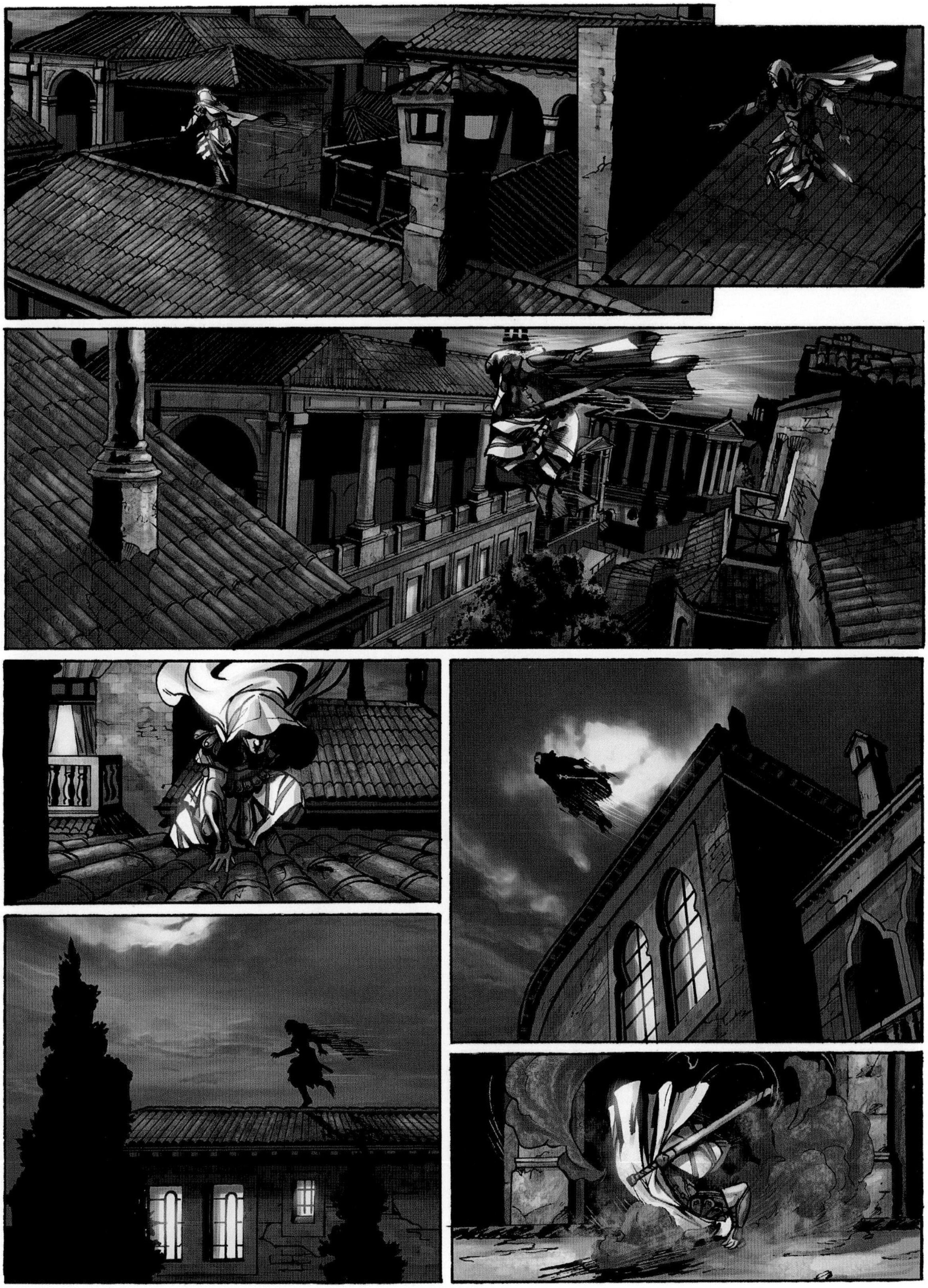

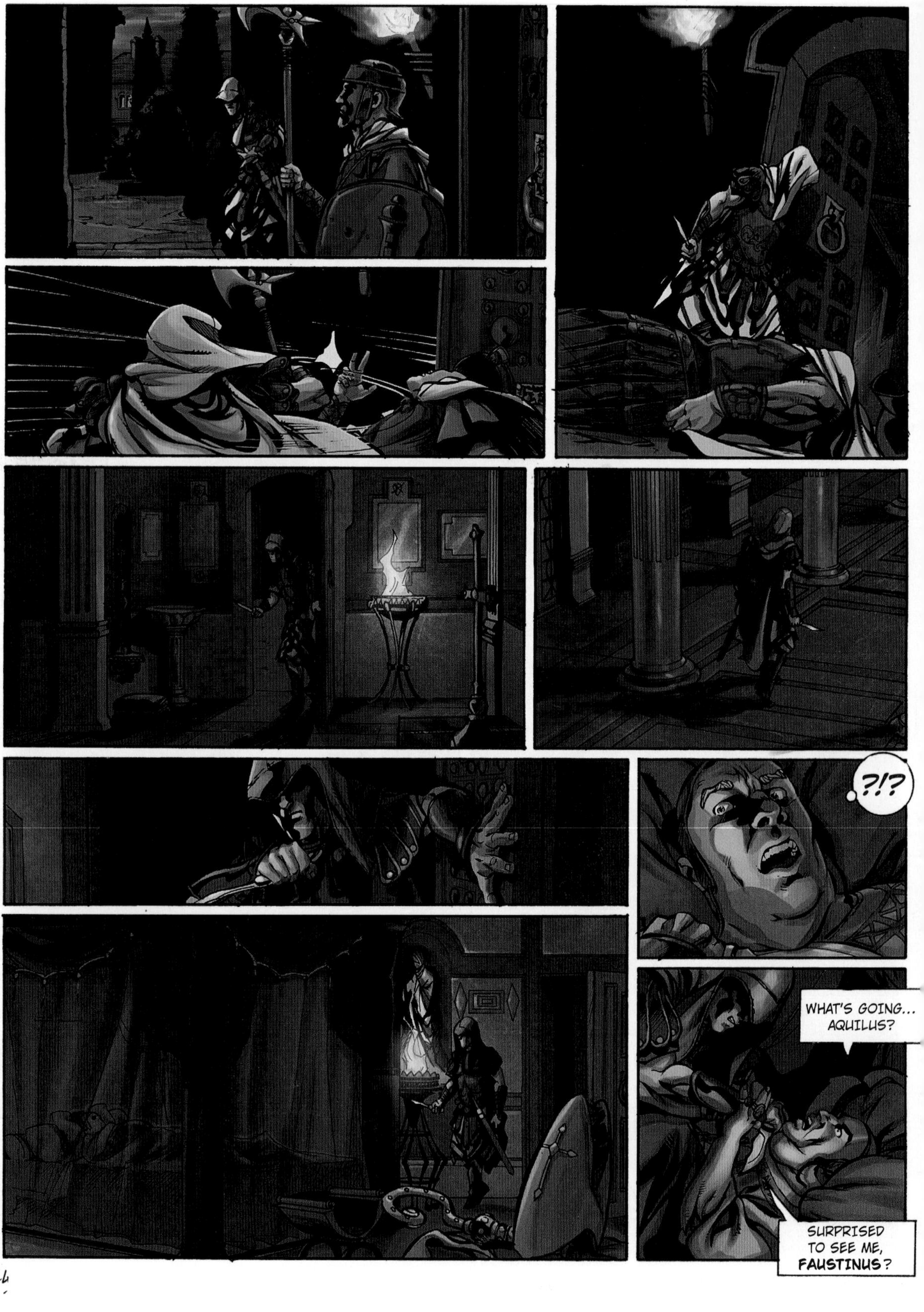
?!?
WHAT'S GOING... AQUILUS?
SURPRISED TO SEE ME, **FAUSTINUS**?

24

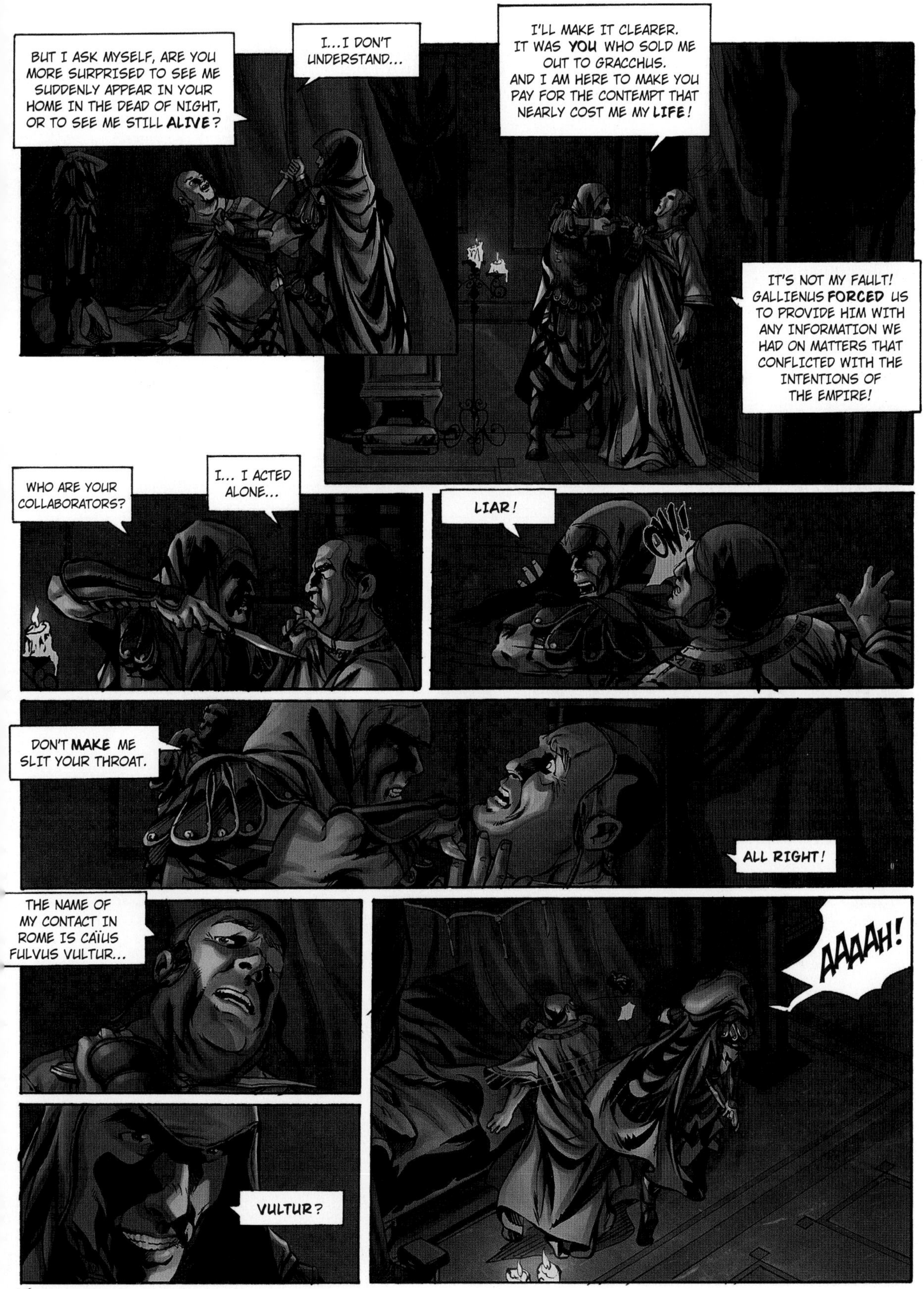

BUT I ASK MYSELF, ARE YOU MORE SURPRISED TO SEE ME SUDDENLY APPEAR IN YOUR HOME IN THE DEAD OF NIGHT, OR TO SEE ME STILL ALIVE?
I...I DON'T UNDERSTAND...
I'LL MAKE IT CLEARER. IT WAS YOU WHO SOLD ME OUT TO GRACCHUS. AND I AM HERE TO MAKE YOU PAY FOR THE CONTEMPT THAT NEARLY COST ME MY LIFE!
IT'S NOT MY FAULT! GALLIENUS FORCED US TO PROVIDE HIM WITH ANY INFORMATION WE HAD ON MATTERS THAT CONFLICTED WITH THE INTENTIONS OF THE EMPIRE!
WHO ARE YOUR COLLABORATORS?
I... I ACTED ALONE...
LIAR!
OW!
DON'T MAKE ME SLIT YOUR THROAT.
ALL RIGHT!
THE NAME OF MY CONTACT IN ROME IS CAÏUS FULVUS VULTUR...
VULTUR?
AAAAH!
25

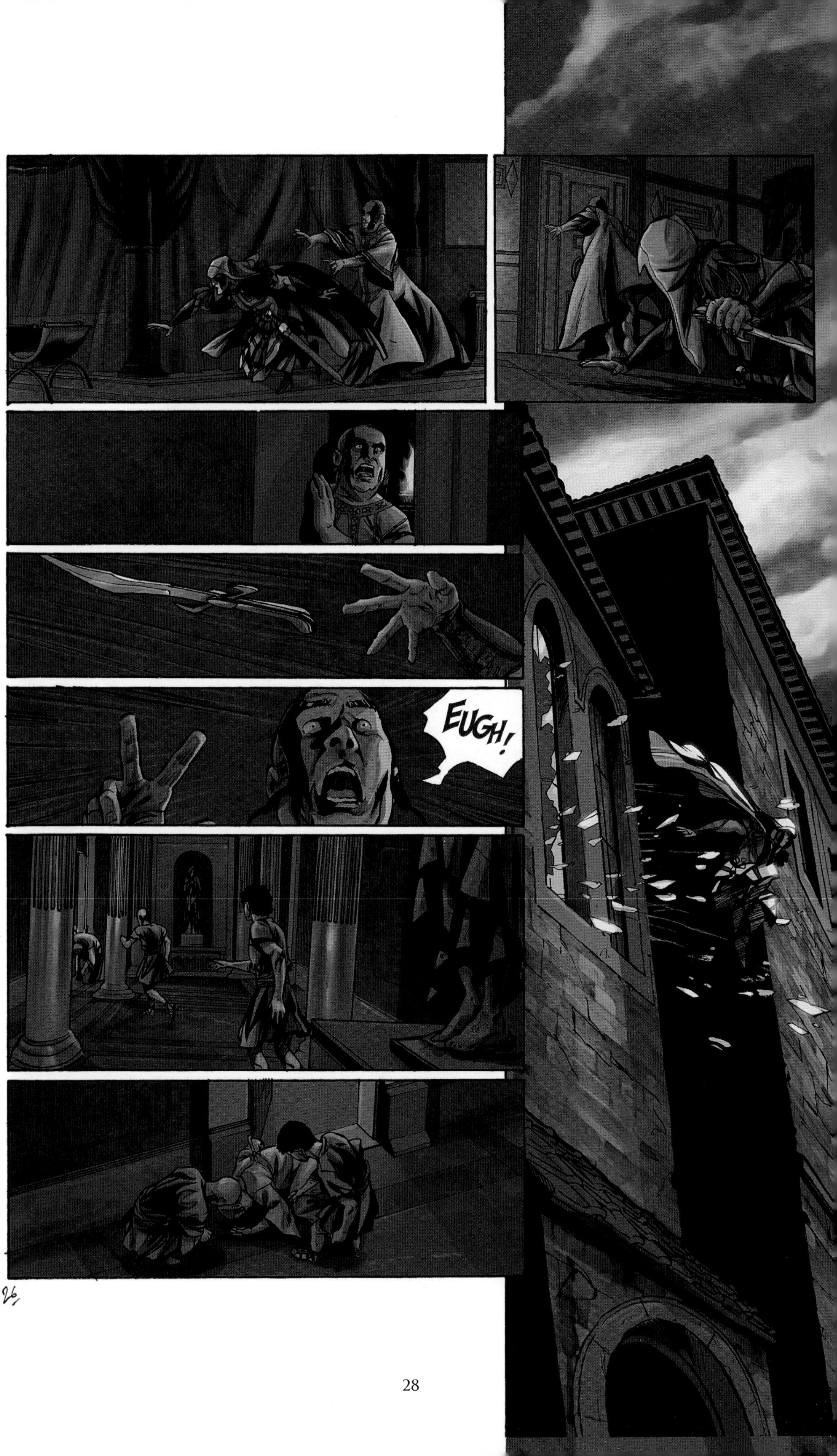
EUGH!

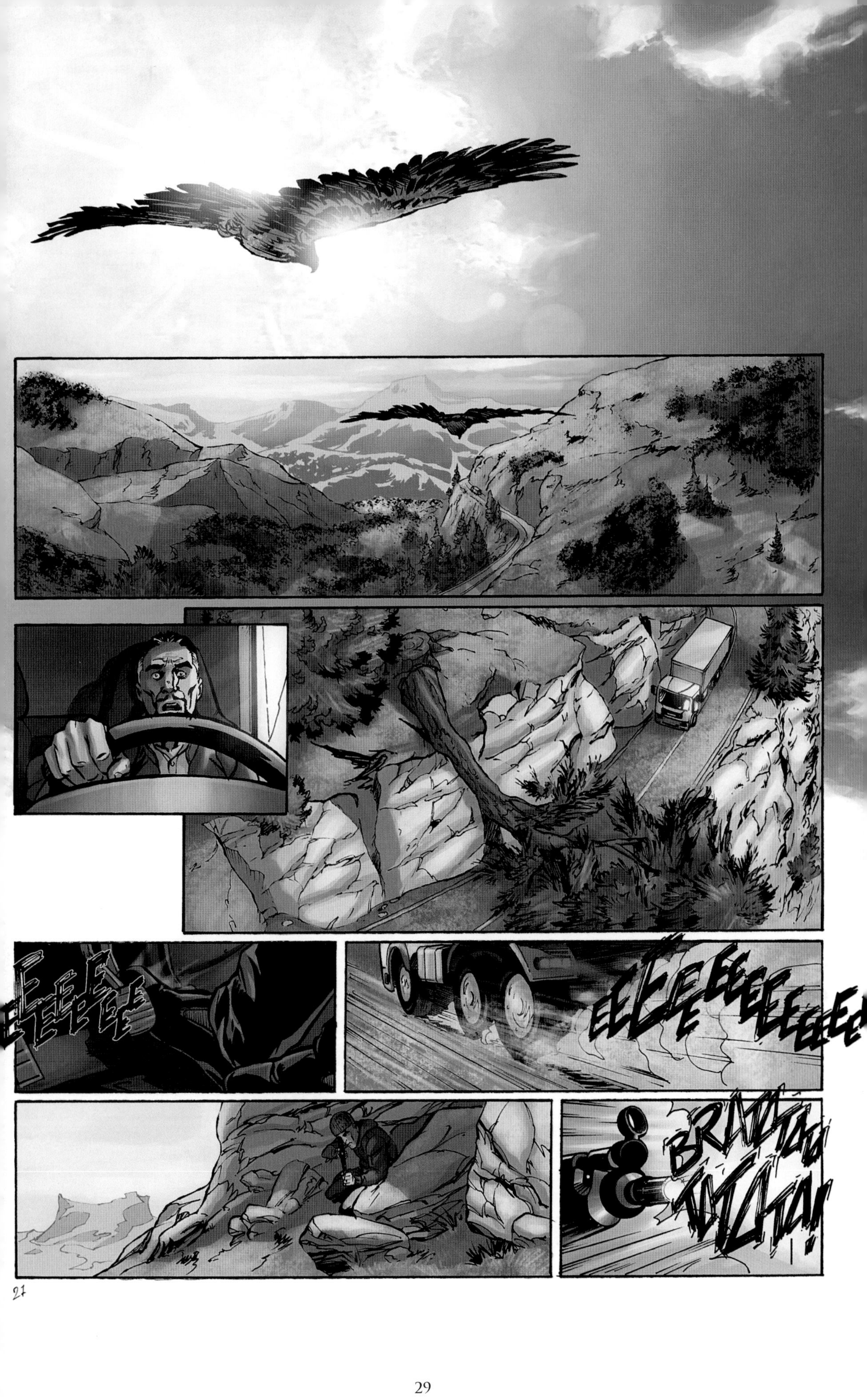

27

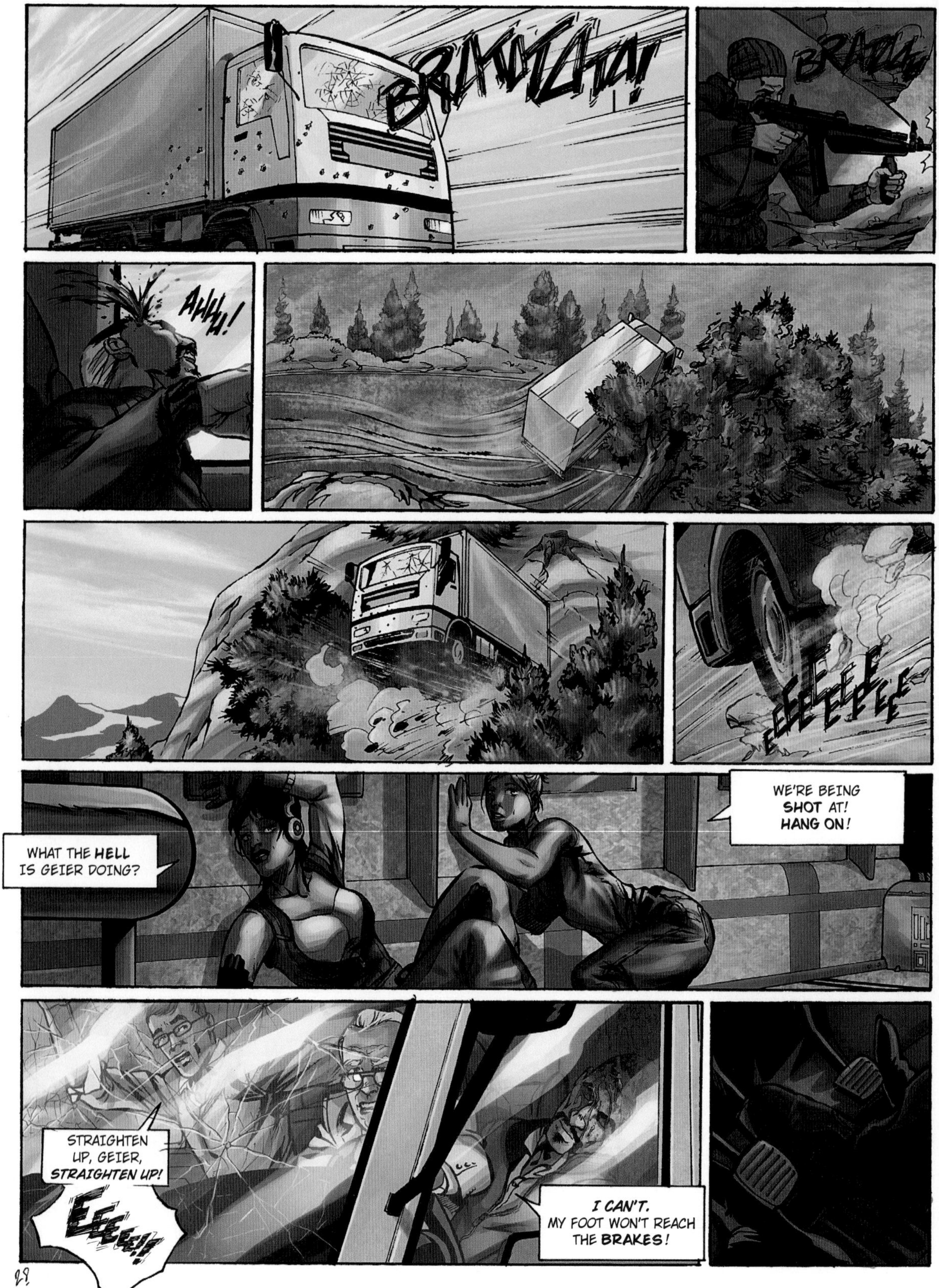

BRAKAKATAK!
AHHH!
WHAT THE HELL IS GEIER DOING?
WE'RE BEING SHOT AT! HANG ON!
STRAIGHTEN UP, GEIER, STRAIGHTEN UP!
EEEEE!!
I CAN'T. MY FOOT WON'T REACH THE BRAKES!

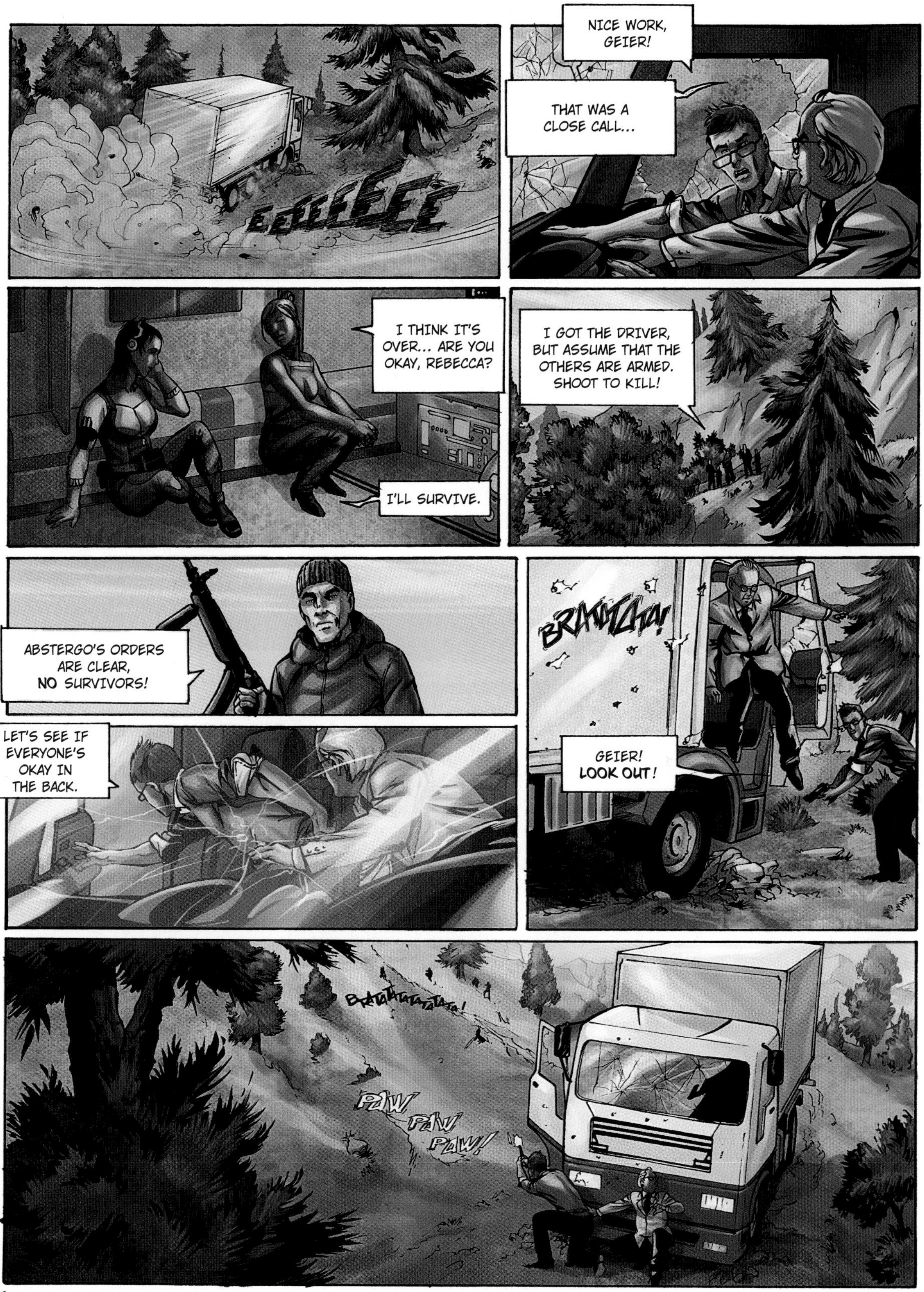
EEEEEEEE
NICE WORK, GEIER!
THAT WAS A CLOSE CALL...
I THINK IT'S OVER... ARE YOU OKAY, REBECCA?
I'LL SURVIVE.
I GOT THE DRIVER, BUT ASSUME THAT THE OTHERS ARE ARMED. SHOOT TO KILL!
ABSTERGO'S ORDERS ARE CLEAR, NO SURVIVORS!
LET'S SEE IF EVERYONE'S OKAY IN THE BACK.
BRAKATCHA!
GEIER! LOOK OUT!
BRATATATATATATA!
PAW PAW PAW!

29

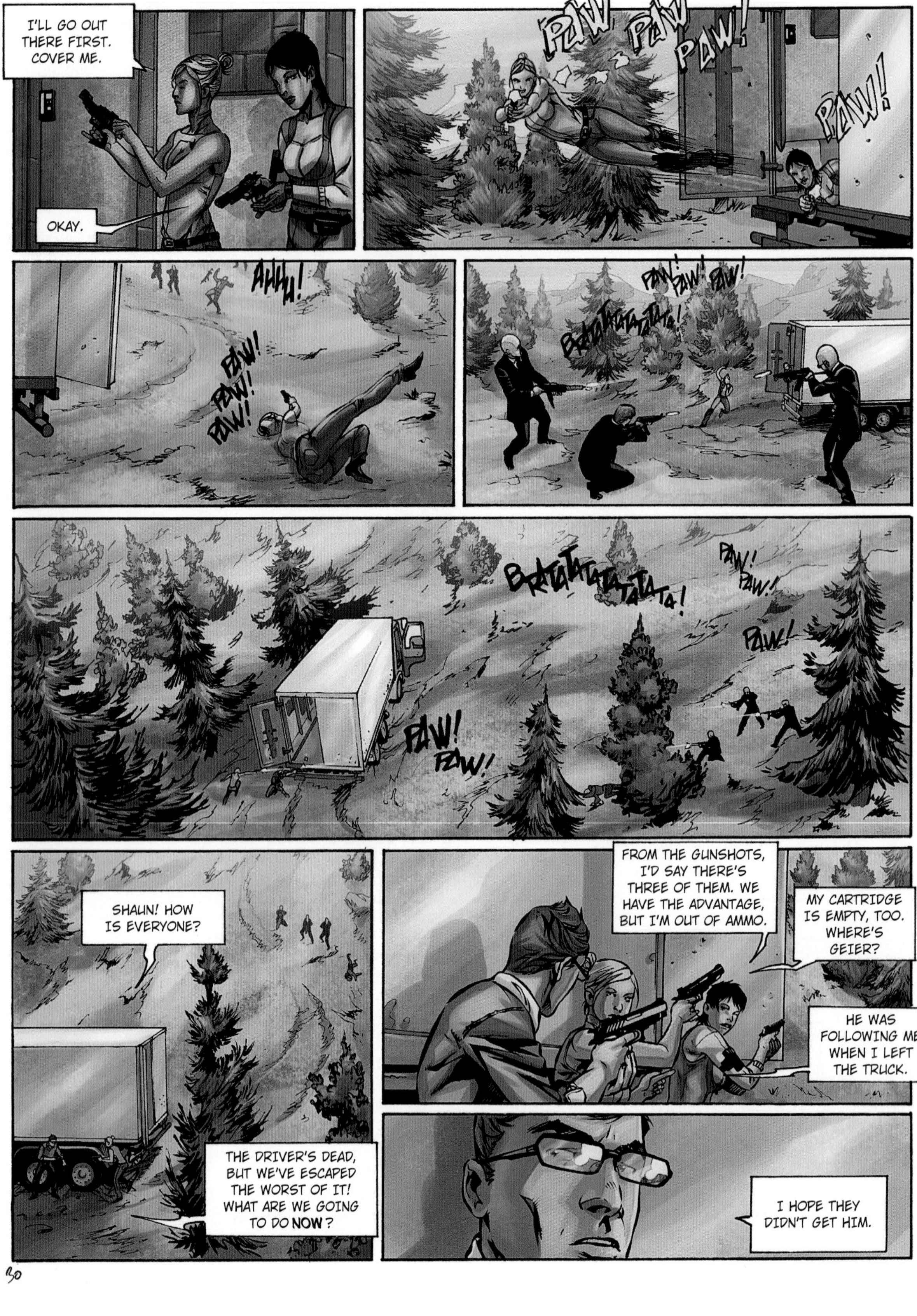

I'LL GO OUT THERE FIRST. COVER ME.
OKAY.
PAW PAW PAW!
PAW!
AHHH!
PAW! PAW! PAW!
PAW! PAW! PAW!
BRATATATATATATA!
BRATATATATATATATA!
PAW! PAW!
PAW!
PAW! PAW!
SHAUN! HOW IS EVERYONE?
THE DRIVER'S DEAD, BUT WE'VE ESCAPED THE WORST OF IT! WHAT ARE WE GOING TO DO **NOW**?
FROM THE GUNSHOTS, I'D SAY THERE'S THREE OF THEM. WE HAVE THE ADVANTAGE, BUT I'M OUT OF AMMO.
MY CARTRIDGE IS EMPTY, TOO. WHERE'S GEIER?
HE WAS FOLLOWING ME WHEN I LEFT THE TRUCK.
I HOPE THEY DIDN'T GET HIM.

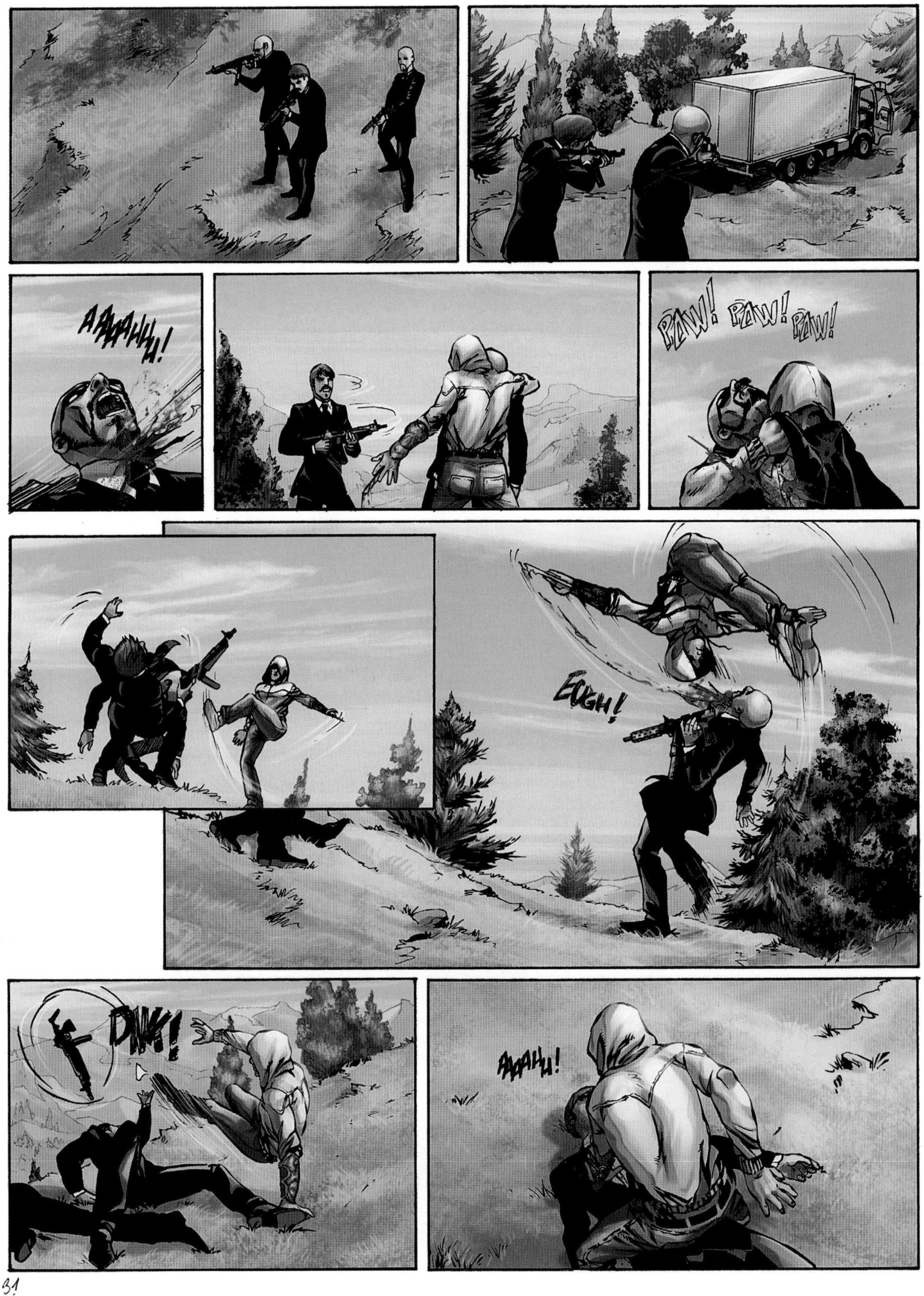
AAAAHHH!
PAW! PAW! PAW!
EUGH!
DNK!
AAAAHH!

31

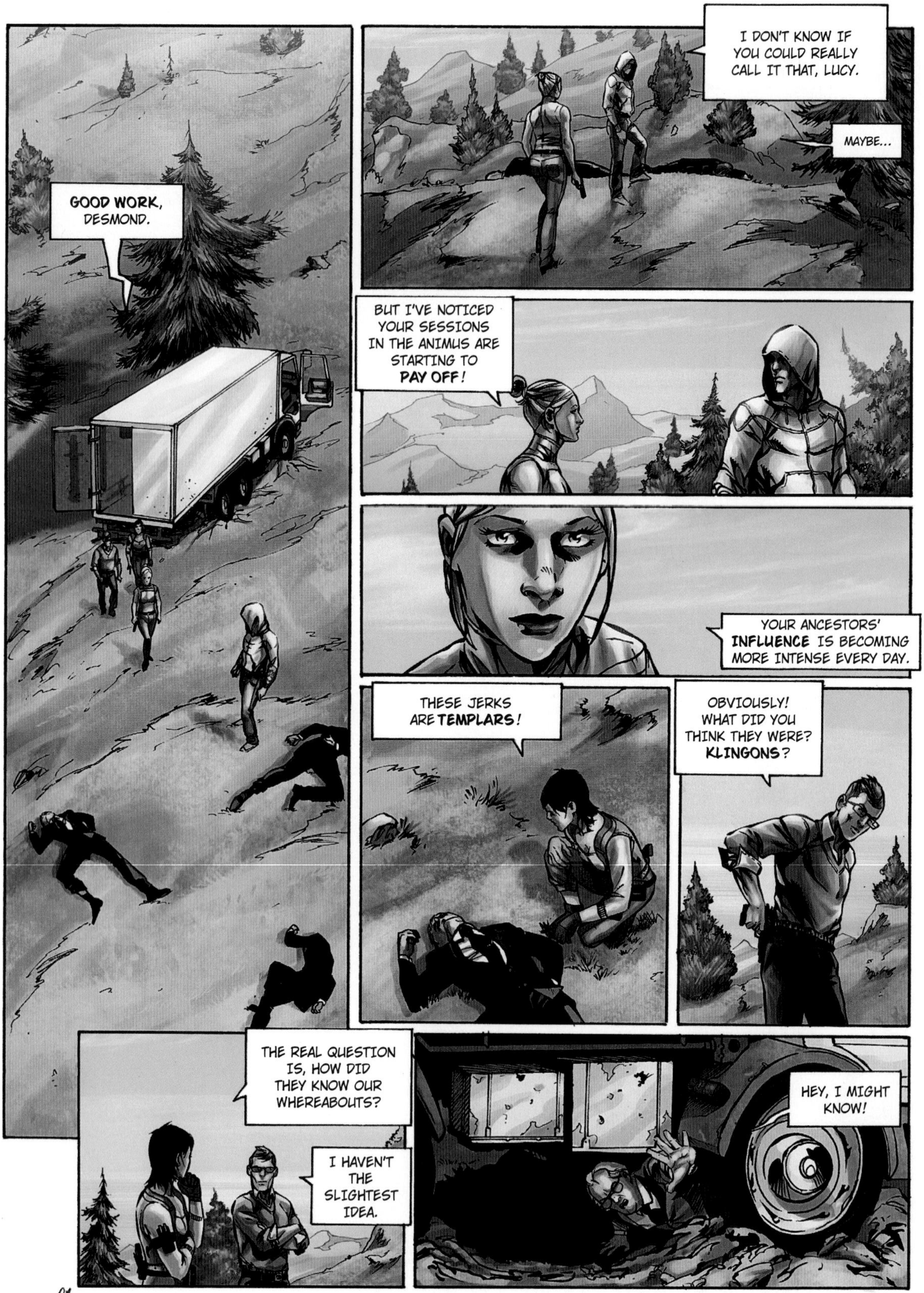
GOOD WORK, DESMOND.
I DON'T KNOW IF YOU COULD REALLY CALL IT THAT, LUCY.
MAYBE...
BUT I'VE NOTICED YOUR SESSIONS IN THE ANIMUS ARE STARTING TO PAY OFF!
YOUR ANCESTORS' INFLUENCE IS BECOMING MORE INTENSE EVERY DAY.
THESE JERKS ARE TEMPLARS!
OBVIOUSLY! WHAT DID YOU THINK THEY WERE? KLINGONS?
THE REAL QUESTION IS, HOW DID THEY KNOW OUR WHEREABOUTS?
I HAVEN'T THE SLIGHTEST IDEA.
HEY, I MIGHT KNOW!

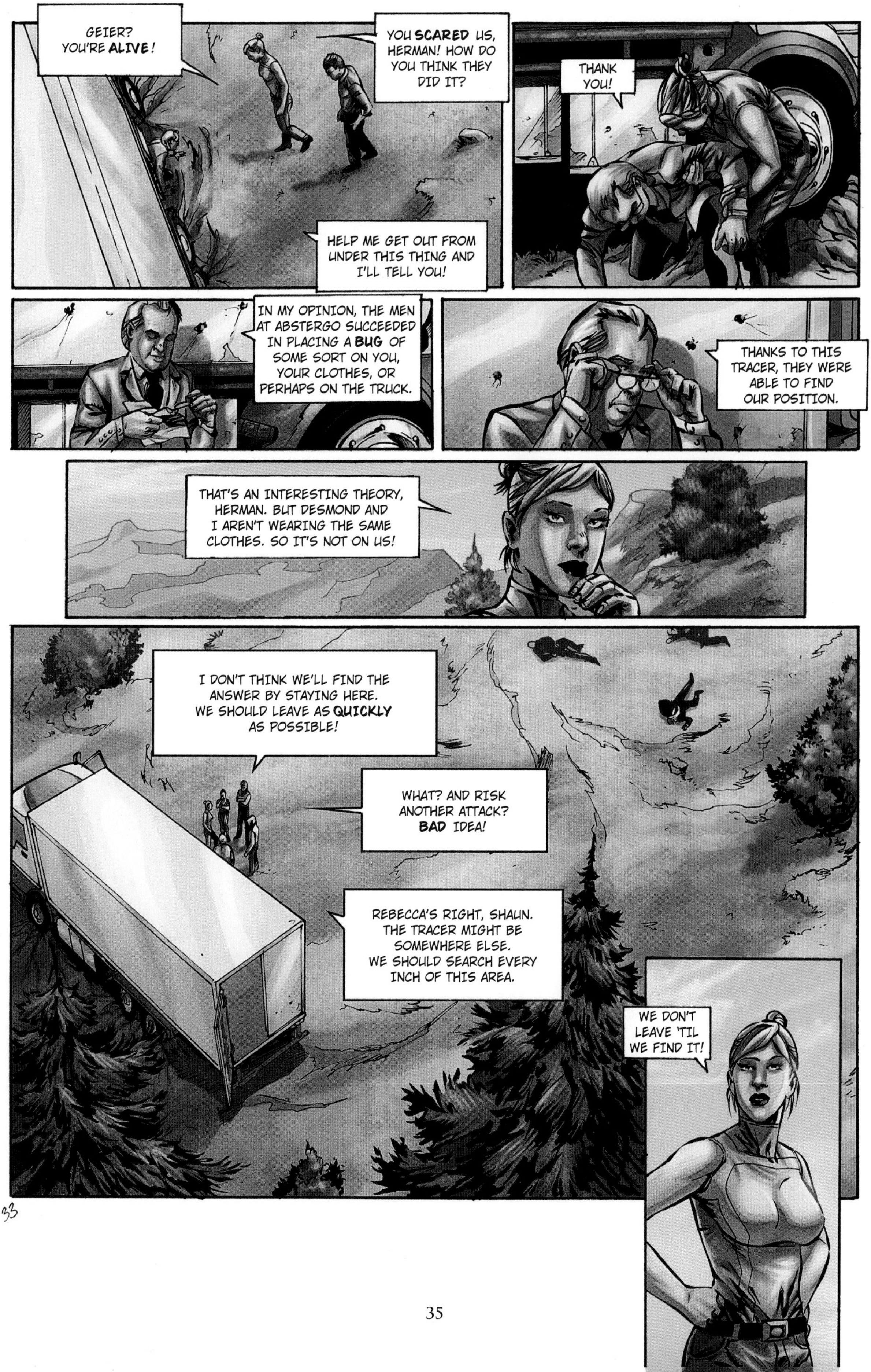
GEIER? YOU'RE ALIVE!
YOU SCARED US, HERMAN! HOW DO YOU THINK THEY DID IT?
HELP ME GET OUT FROM UNDER THIS THING AND I'LL TELL YOU!
THANK YOU!
IN MY OPINION, THE MEN AT ABSTERGO SUCCEEDED IN PLACING A BUG OF SOME SORT ON YOU, YOUR CLOTHES, OR PERHAPS ON THE TRUCK.
THANKS TO THIS TRACER, THEY WERE ABLE TO FIND OUR POSITION.
THAT'S AN INTERESTING THEORY, HERMAN. BUT DESMOND AND I AREN'T WEARING THE SAME CLOTHES. SO IT'S NOT ON US!
I DON'T THINK WE'LL FIND THE ANSWER BY STAYING HERE. WE SHOULD LEAVE AS QUICKLY AS POSSIBLE!
WHAT? AND RISK ANOTHER ATTACK? BAD IDEA!
REBECCA'S RIGHT, SHAUN. THE TRACER MIGHT BE SOMEWHERE ELSE. WE SHOULD SEARCH EVERY INCH OF THIS AREA.
WE DON'T LEAVE 'TIL WE FIND IT!

33

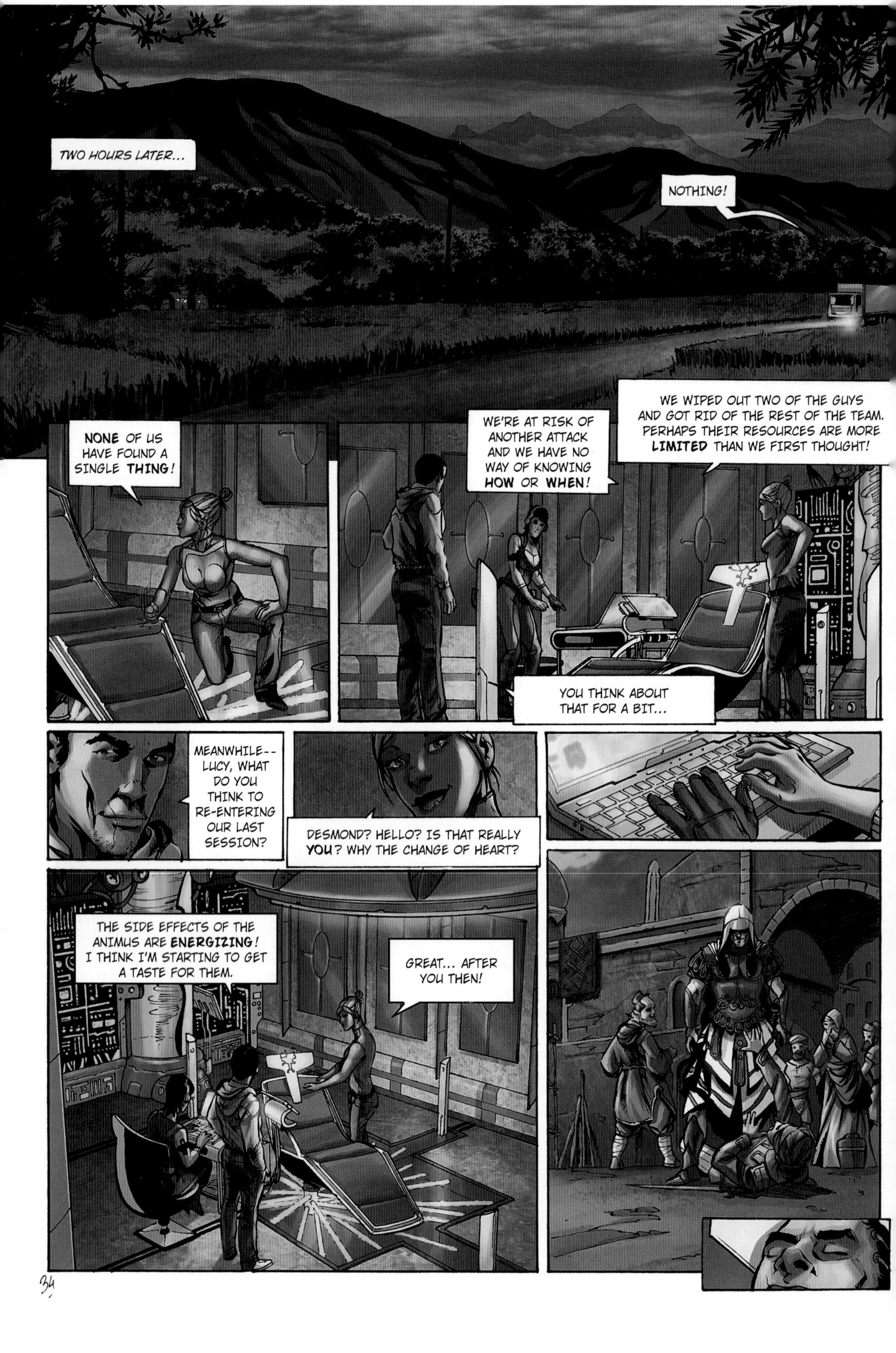
TWO HOURS LATER...
NOTHING!
NONE OF US HAVE FOUND A SINGLE THING!
WE'RE AT RISK OF ANOTHER ATTACK AND WE HAVE NO WAY OF KNOWING HOW OR WHEN!
WE WIPED OUT TWO OF THE GUYS AND GOT RID OF THE REST OF THE TEAM. PERHAPS THEIR RESOURCES ARE MORE LIMITED THAN WE FIRST THOUGHT!
YOU THINK ABOUT THAT FOR A BIT...
MEANWHILE-- LUCY, WHAT DO YOU THINK TO RE-ENTERING OUR LAST SESSION?
DESMOND? HELLO? IS THAT REALLY YOU? WHY THE CHANGE OF HEART?
THE SIDE EFFECTS OF THE ANIMUS ARE ENERGIZING! I THINK I'M STARTING TO GET A TASTE FOR THEM.
GREAT... AFTER YOU THEN!
34

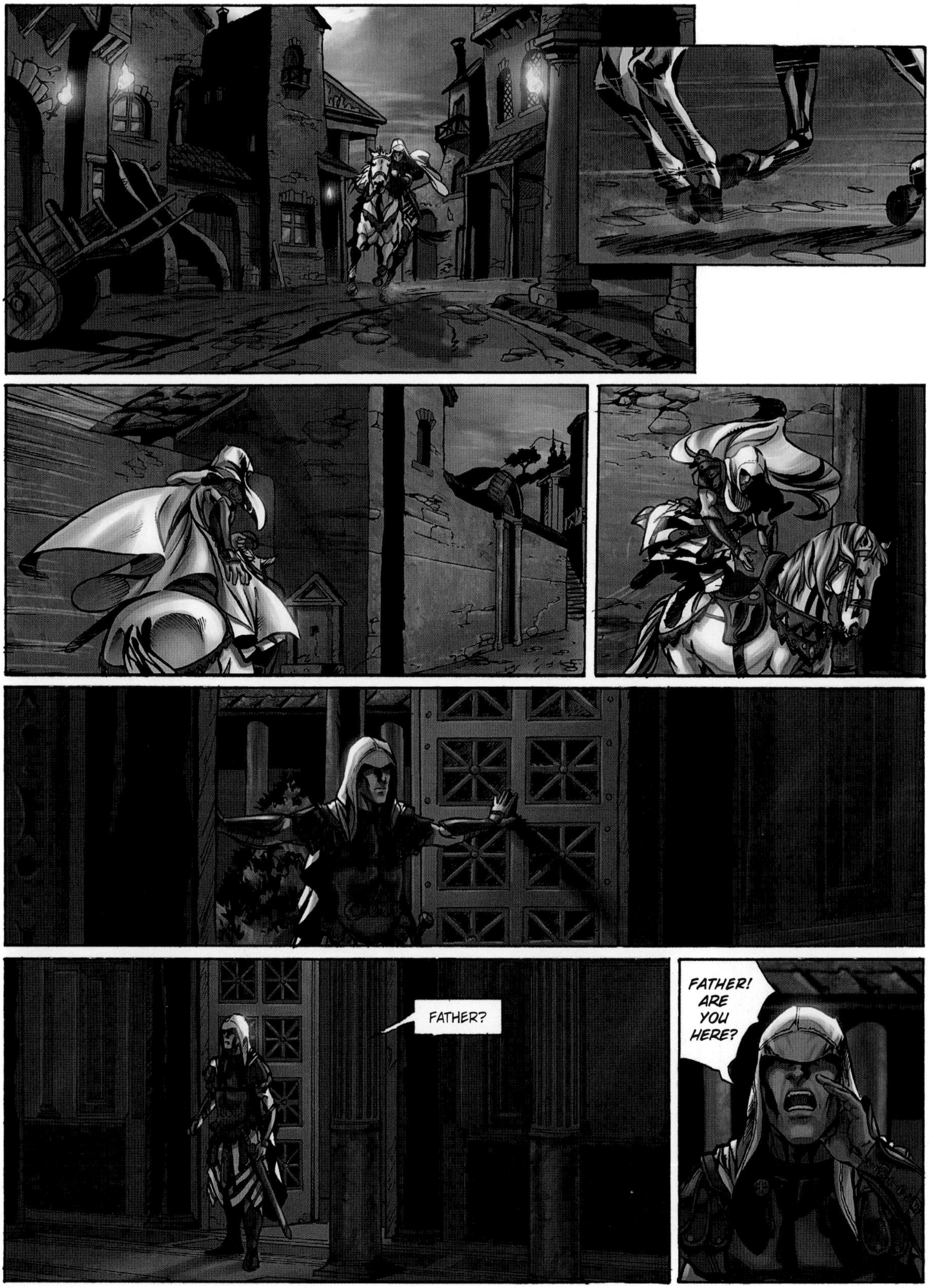
FATHER?
FATHER! ARE YOU HERE?
35

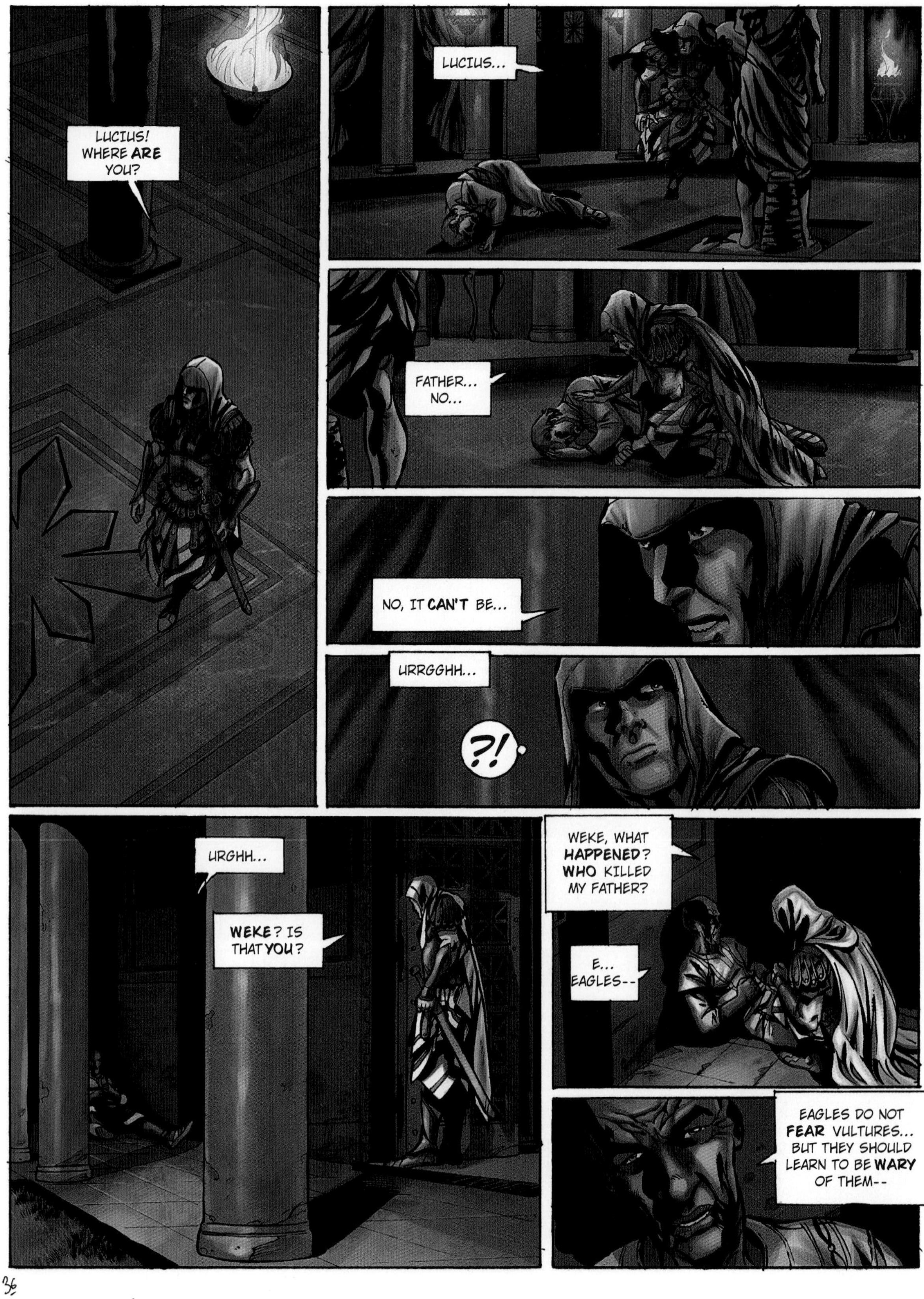
LUCIUS!
WHERE **ARE** YOU?
LUCIUS...
FATHER... NO...
NO, IT **CAN'T** BE...
URRGGHH...
?!
URGHH...
WEKE? IS THAT **YOU**?
WEKE, WHAT **HAPPENED**? **WHO** KILLED MY FATHER?
E... EAGLES--
EAGLES DO NOT **FEAR** VULTURES... BUT THEY SHOULD LEARN TO BE **WARY** OF THEM--

WEKE! WHAT DO YOU MEAN?

WEKE!

THE SENATOR HAS RUN AWAY, AQUILLUS...

THEY ARGUED AND THEN I HEARD YOUR FATHER **CRY OUT** --

WHEN I GOT DOWN THERE TO SEE WHAT HAD HAPPENED, LUCIUS WAS DEAD. WEKE **LAUNCHED HIMSELF** IN PURSUIT OF THE SENATOR.

WHAT HAPPENED?

AFTER YOU LEFT, YOUR FATHER REMAINED IN THE GARDEN.

"NOT LONG AFTER, I HEARD SENATOR VULTUR LEAVE HIS ROOM AND REJOIN LUCIUS.

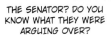

THE SENATOR? DO YOU KNOW WHAT THEY WERE ARGUING OVER?

IT WASN'T VERY CLEAR. BUT APPARENTLY, THE SENATOR DESIRED AN OBJECT THAT YOUR FATHER REFUSED TO HAND OVER TO HIM.

DO YOU KNOW WHAT **BECAME** OF THIS OBJECT?

WEKE TRIED TO TAKE IT BACK FROM HIM, BUT THE SENATOR DEFENDED HIMSELF AND **KILLED** WEKE.

37

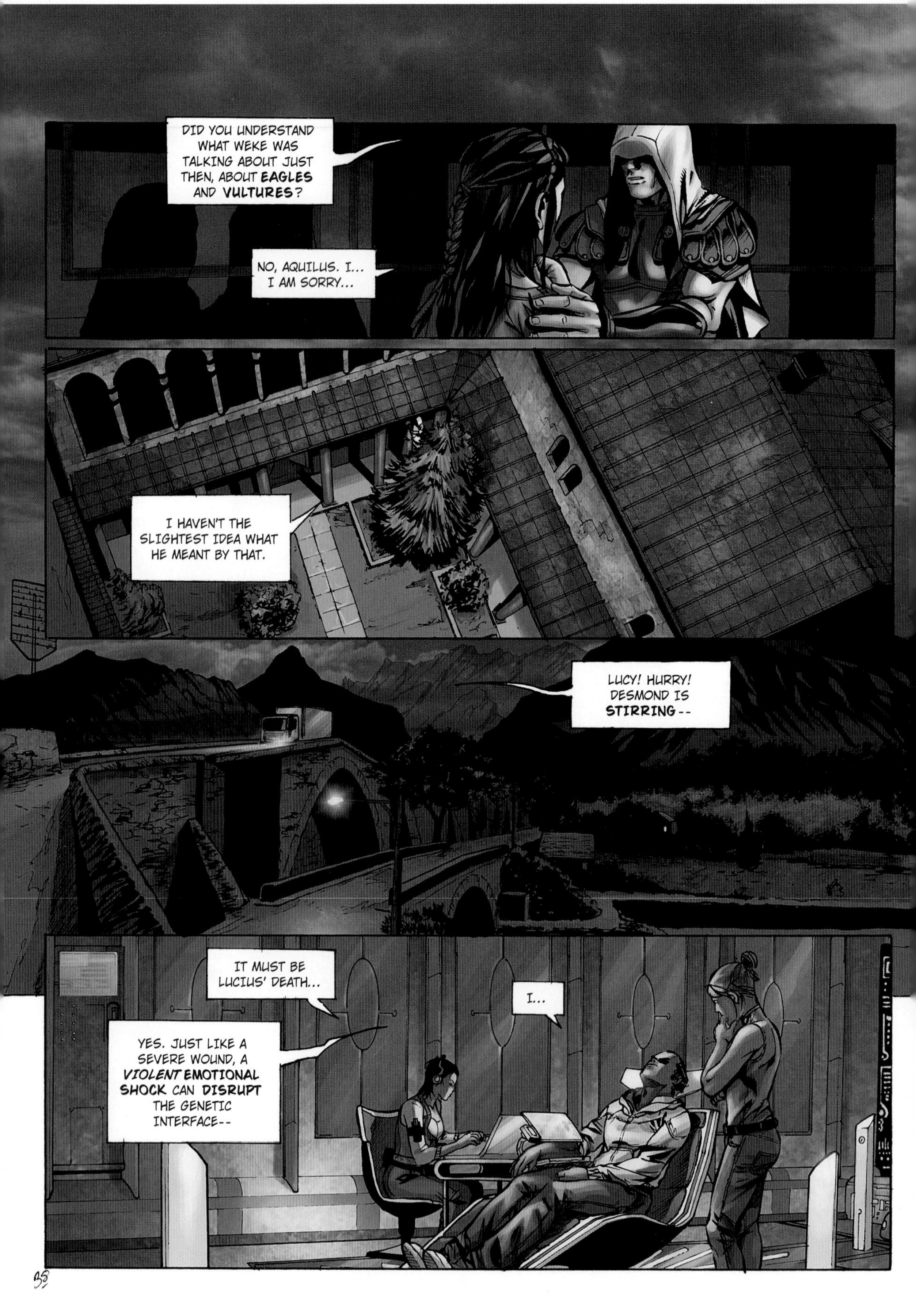
DID YOU UNDERSTAND WHAT WEKE WAS TALKING ABOUT JUST THEN, ABOUT **EAGLES** AND **VULTURES**?
NO, AQUILUS. I... I AM SORRY...
I HAVEN'T THE SLIGHTEST IDEA WHAT HE MEANT BY THAT.
LUCY! HURRY! DESMOND IS **STIRRING**--
IT MUST BE LUCIUS' DEATH...
YES. JUST LIKE A SEVERE WOUND, A ***VIOLENT*** **EMOTIONAL SHOCK** CAN **DISRUPT** THE GENETIC INTERFACE--
I...

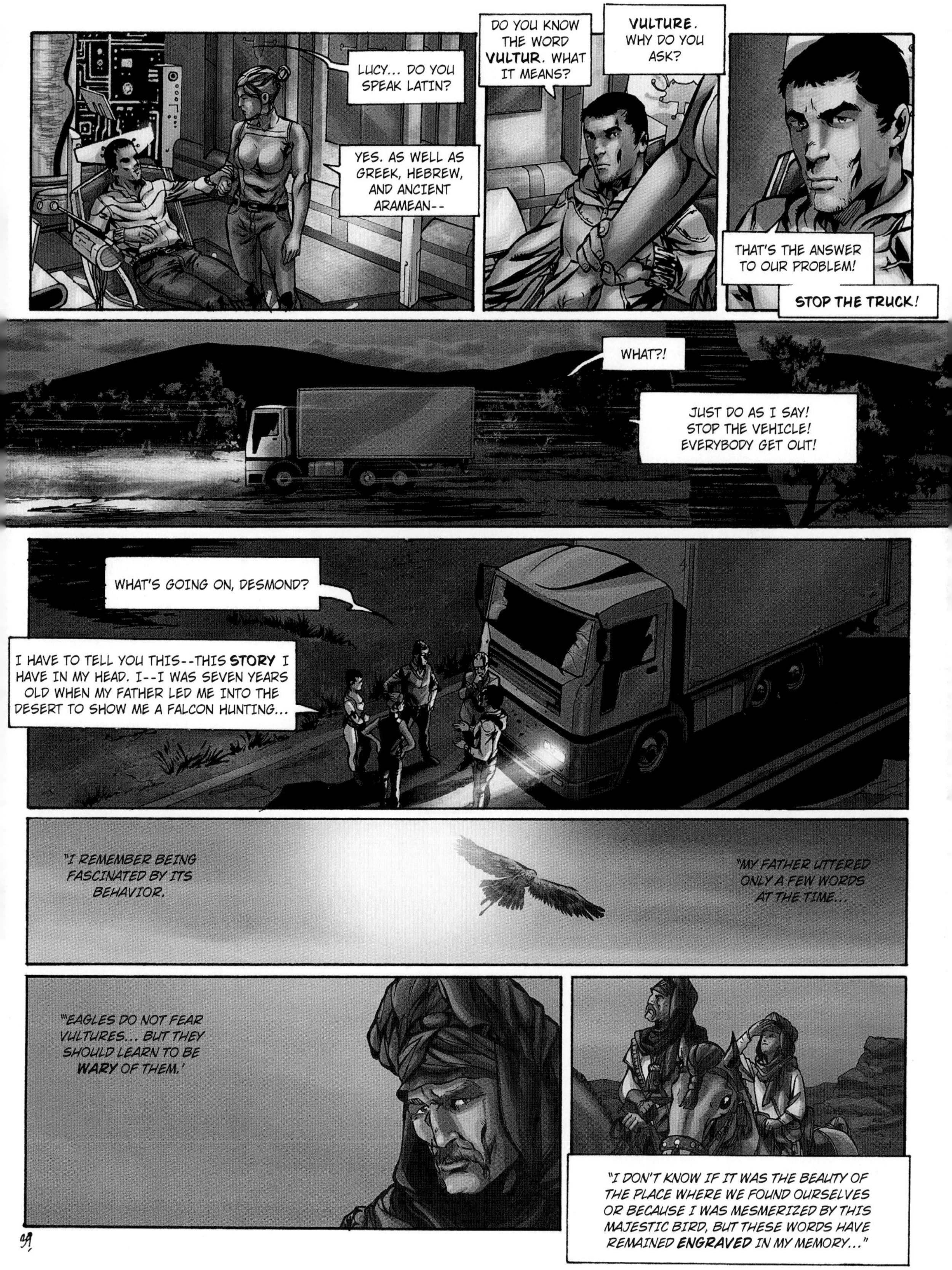
LUCY... DO YOU SPEAK LATIN?
YES. AS WELL AS GREEK, HEBREW, AND ANCIENT ARAMEAN--
DO YOU KNOW THE WORD VULTUR. WHAT IT MEANS?
VULTURE. WHY DO YOU ASK?
THAT'S THE ANSWER TO OUR PROBLEM!
STOP THE TRUCK!
WHAT?!
JUST DO AS I SAY! STOP THE VEHICLE! EVERYBODY GET OUT!
WHAT'S GOING ON, DESMOND?
I HAVE TO TELL YOU THIS--THIS STORY I HAVE IN MY HEAD. I--I WAS SEVEN YEARS OLD WHEN MY FATHER LED ME INTO THE DESERT TO SHOW ME A FALCON HUNTING...
"I REMEMBER BEING FASCINATED BY ITS BEHAVIOR.
"MY FATHER UTTERED ONLY A FEW WORDS AT THE TIME...
"EAGLES DO NOT FEAR VULTURES... BUT THEY SHOULD LEARN TO BE WARY OF THEM.'
"I DON'T KNOW IF IT WAS THE BEAUTY OF THE PLACE WHERE WE FOUND OURSELVES OR BECAUSE I WAS MESMERIZED BY THIS MAJESTIC BIRD, BUT THESE WORDS HAVE REMAINED ENGRAVED IN MY MEMORY..."

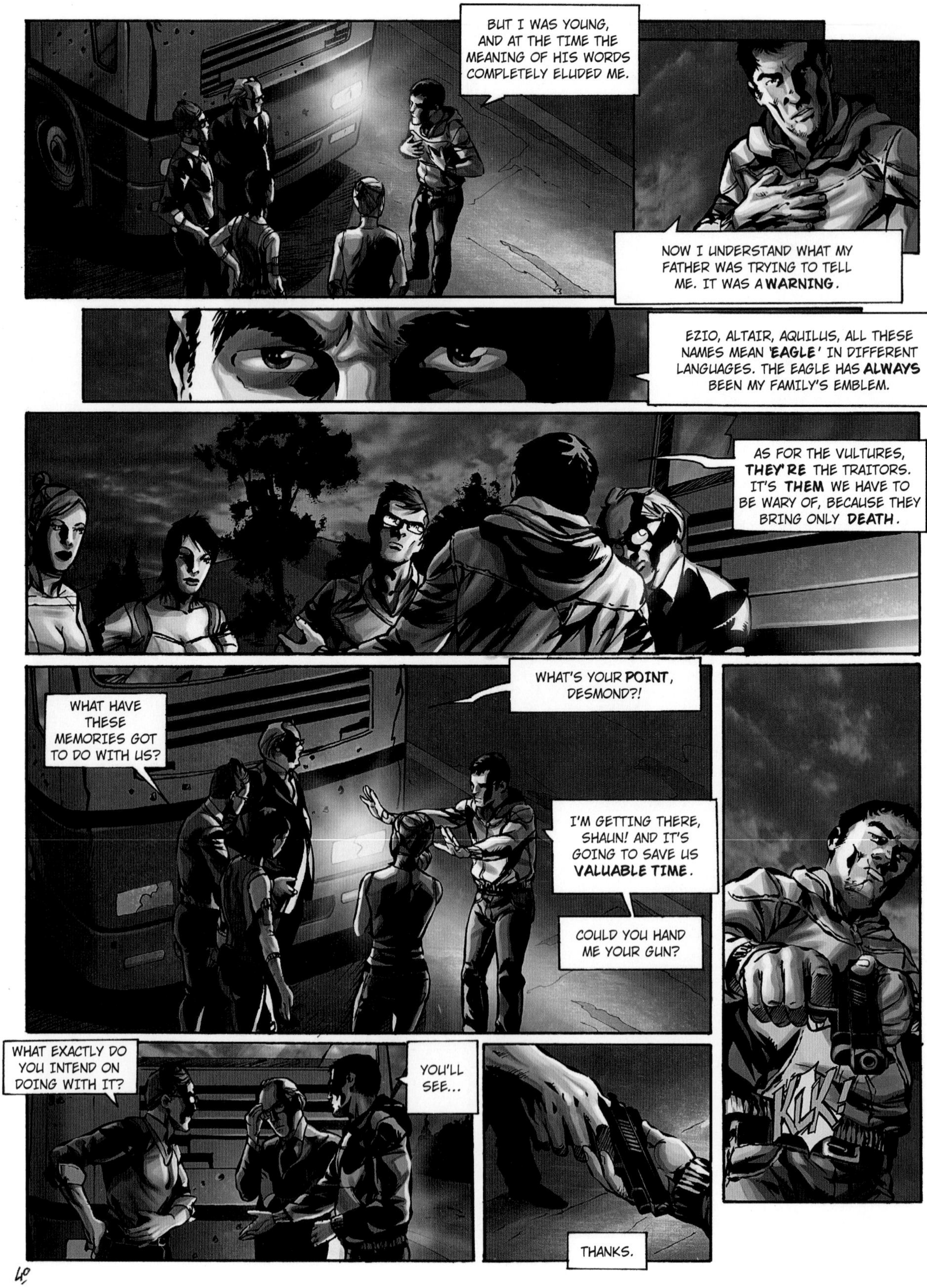

BUT I WAS YOUNG, AND AT THE TIME THE MEANING OF HIS WORDS COMPLETELY ELUDED ME.
NOW I UNDERSTAND WHAT MY FATHER WAS TRYING TO TELL ME. IT WAS A WARNING.
EZIO, ALTAIR, AQUILUS, ALL THESE NAMES MEAN 'EAGLE' IN DIFFERENT LANGUAGES. THE EAGLE HAS ALWAYS BEEN MY FAMILY'S EMBLEM.
AS FOR THE VULTURES, THEY'RE THE TRAITORS. IT'S THEM WE HAVE TO BE WARY OF, BECAUSE THEY BRING ONLY DEATH.
WHAT'S YOUR POINT, DESMOND?!
WHAT HAVE THESE MEMORIES GOT TO DO WITH US?
I'M GETTING THERE, SHAUN! AND IT'S GOING TO SAVE US VALUABLE TIME.
COULD YOU HAND ME YOUR GUN?
KLIK!
WHAT EXACTLY DO YOU INTEND ON DOING WITH IT?
YOU'LL SEE...
THANKS.

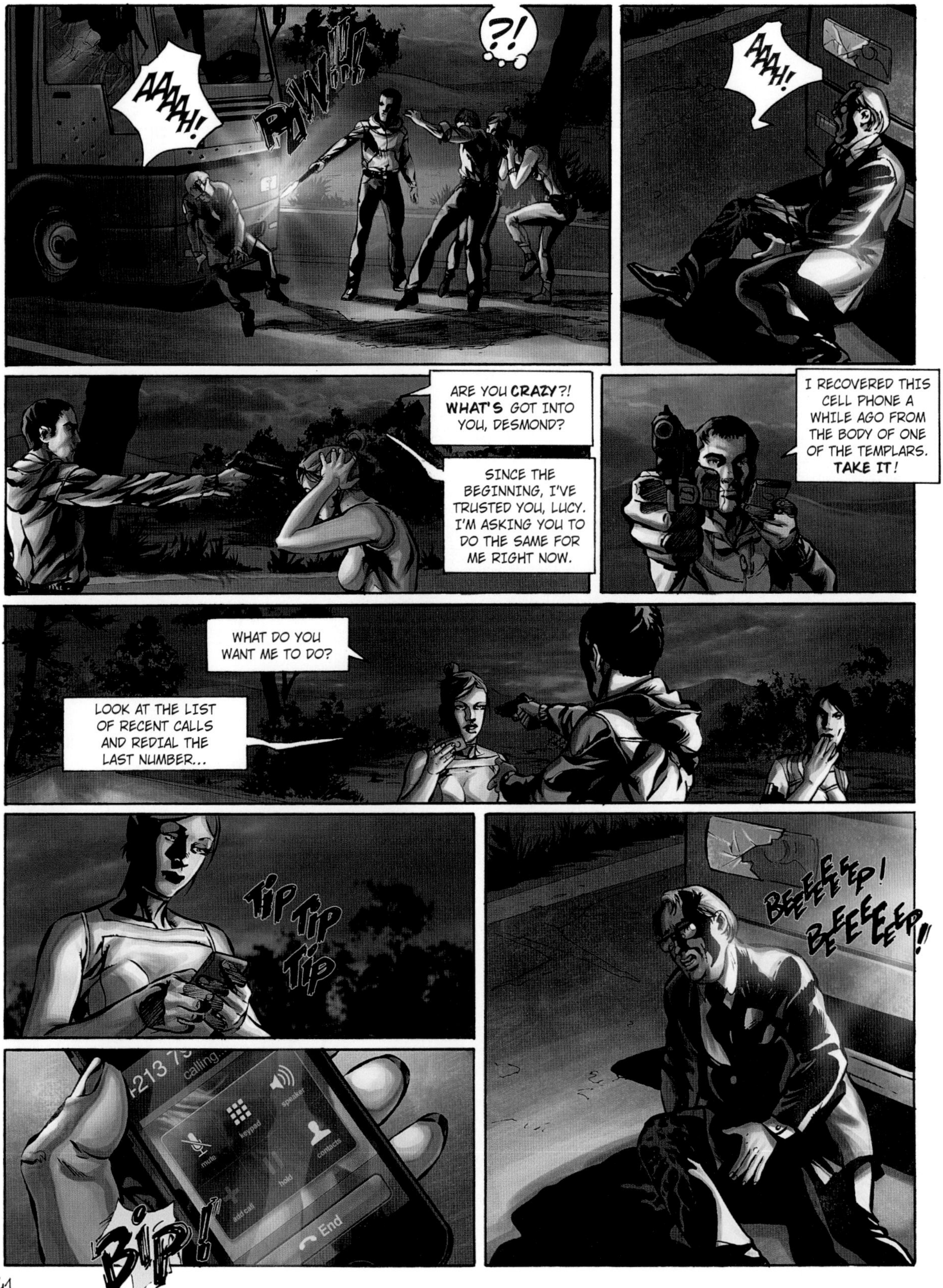

AAAAH!
PAWWW!!!
?!
AAAH!
ARE YOU CRAZY?! WHAT'S GOT INTO YOU, DESMOND?
SINCE THE BEGINNING, I'VE TRUSTED YOU, LUCY. I'M ASKING YOU TO DO THE SAME FOR ME RIGHT NOW.
I RECOVERED THIS CELL PHONE A WHILE AGO FROM THE BODY OF ONE OF THE TEMPLARS. TAKE IT!
WHAT DO YOU WANT ME TO DO?
LOOK AT THE LIST OF RECENT CALLS AND REDIAL THE LAST NUMBER...
TIP TIP TIP
calling...
mute
keypad
speaker
contacts
add call
hold
End
BIP!
BEEEEEEP! BEEEEEEP!!

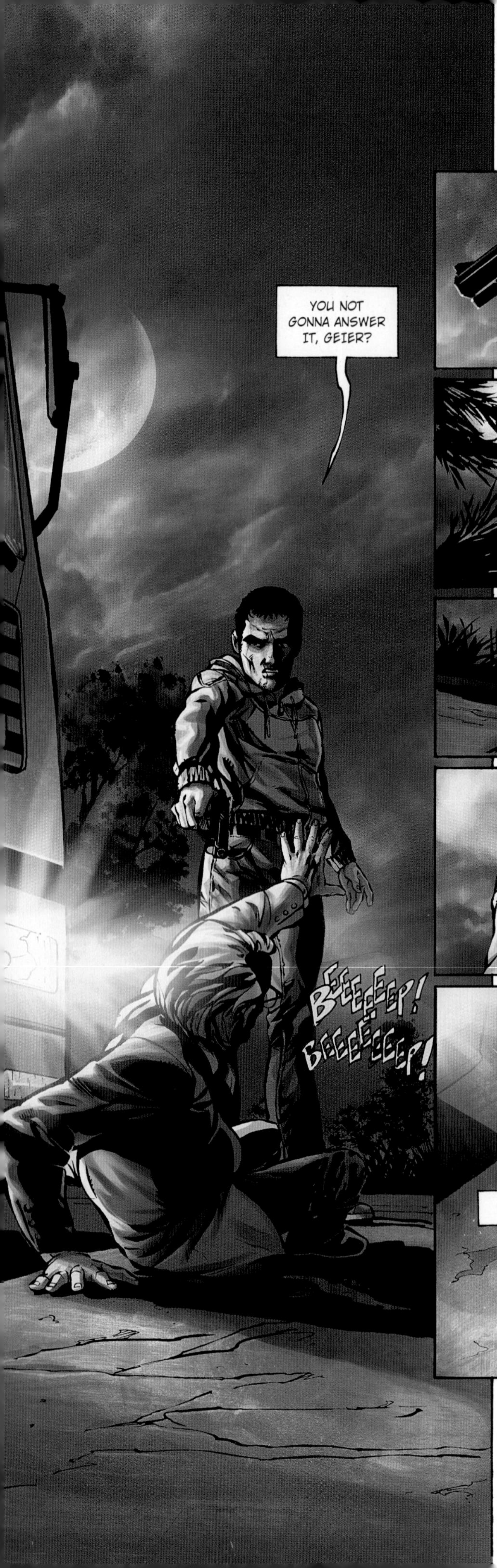
YOU NOT GONNA ANSWER IT, GEIER?
BEEEEEEEP!
BEEEEEEEEP!

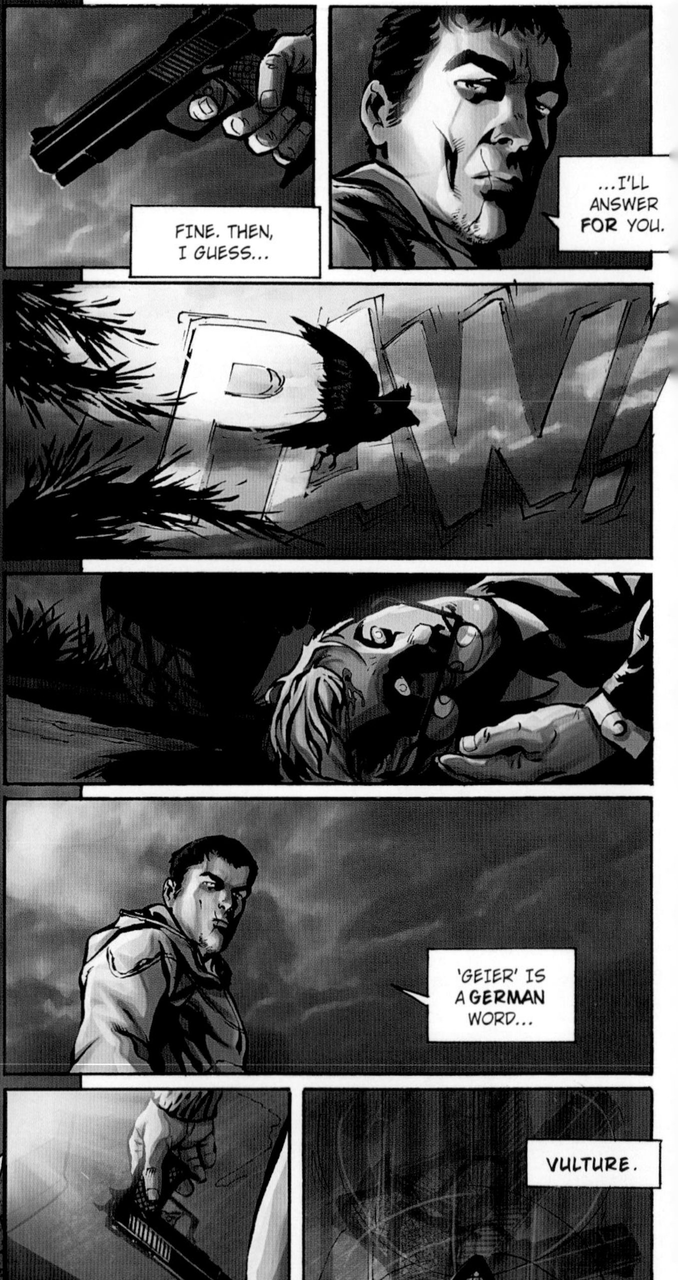
FINE. THEN, I GUESS...
...I'LL ANSWER **FOR** YOU.
BLAM!
'GEIER' IS A **GERMAN** WORD...
IT MEANS...
VULTURE.

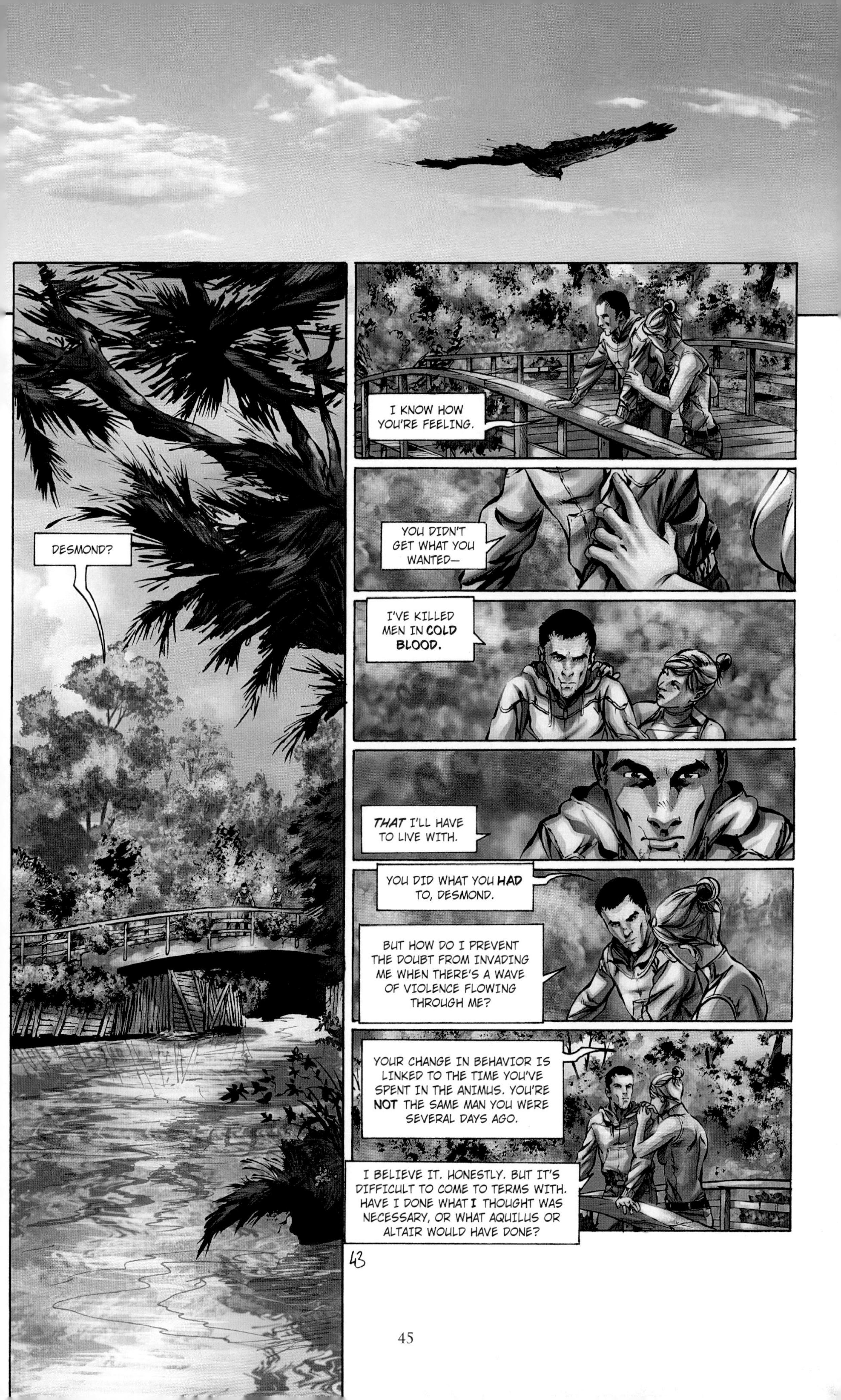
DESMOND?
I KNOW HOW YOU'RE FEELING.
YOU DIDN'T GET WHAT YOU WANTED—
I'VE KILLED MEN IN COLD BLOOD.
THAT I'LL HAVE TO LIVE WITH.
YOU DID WHAT YOU HAD TO, DESMOND.
BUT HOW DO I PREVENT THE DOUBT FROM INVADING ME WHEN THERE'S A WAVE OF VIOLENCE FLOWING THROUGH ME?
YOUR CHANGE IN BEHAVIOR IS LINKED TO THE TIME YOU'VE SPENT IN THE ANIMUS. YOU'RE NOT THE SAME MAN YOU WERE SEVERAL DAYS AGO.
I BELIEVE IT. HONESTLY. BUT IT'S DIFFICULT TO COME TO TERMS WITH. HAVE I DONE WHAT I THOUGHT WAS NECESSARY, OR WHAT AQUILUS OR ALTAIR WOULD HAVE DONE?
43

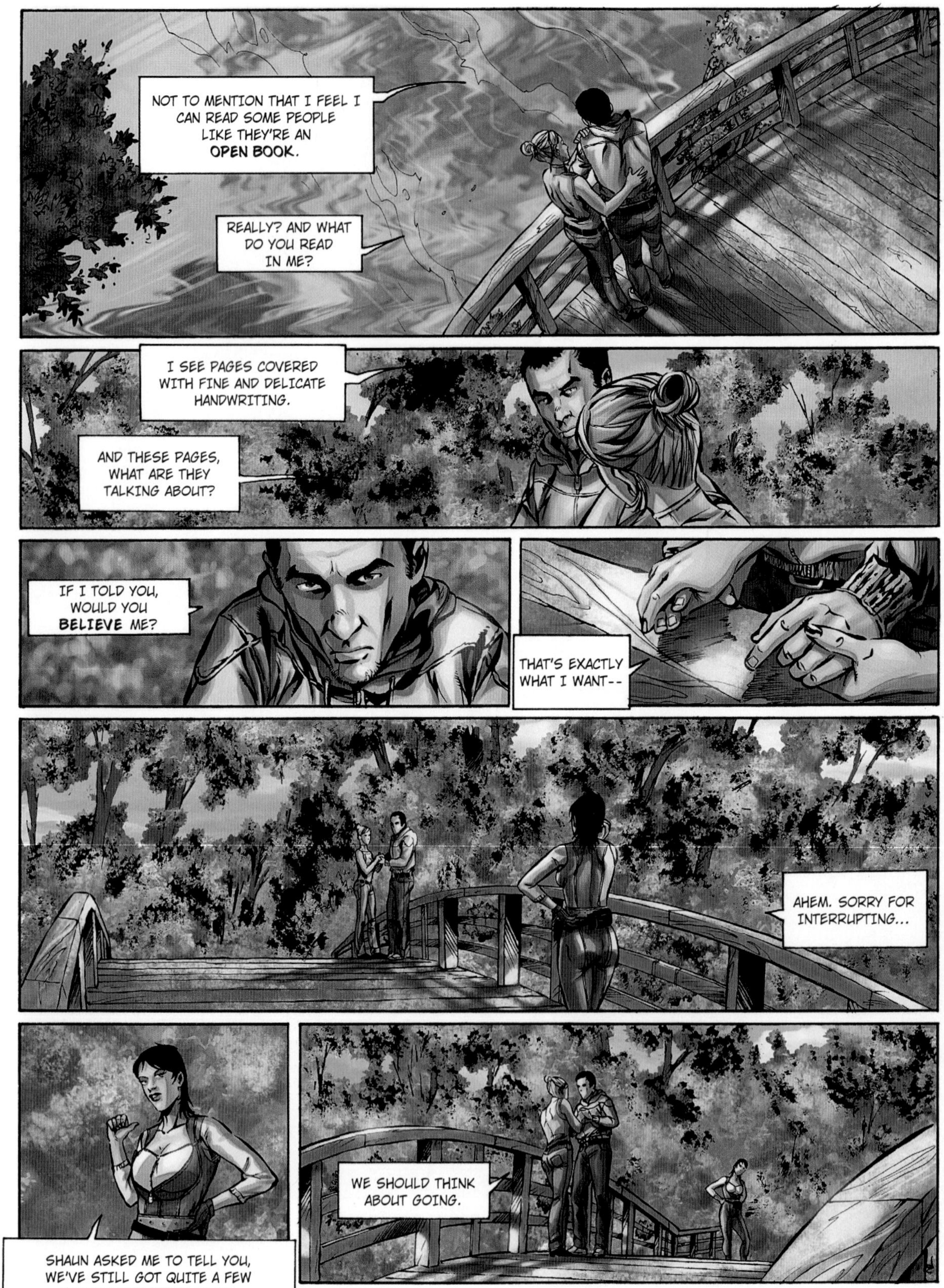
NOT TO MENTION THAT I FEEL I CAN READ SOME PEOPLE LIKE THEY'RE AN **OPEN BOOK**.
REALLY? AND WHAT DO YOU READ IN ME?
I SEE PAGES COVERED WITH FINE AND DELICATE HANDWRITING.
AND THESE PAGES, WHAT ARE THEY TALKING ABOUT?
IF I TOLD YOU, WOULD YOU **BELIEVE** ME?
THAT'S EXACTLY WHAT I WANT--
AHEM. SORRY FOR INTERRUPTING...
SHAUN ASKED ME TO TELL YOU, WE'VE STILL GOT QUITE A FEW HOURS LEFT AHEAD OF US.
WE SHOULD THINK ABOUT GOING.
44

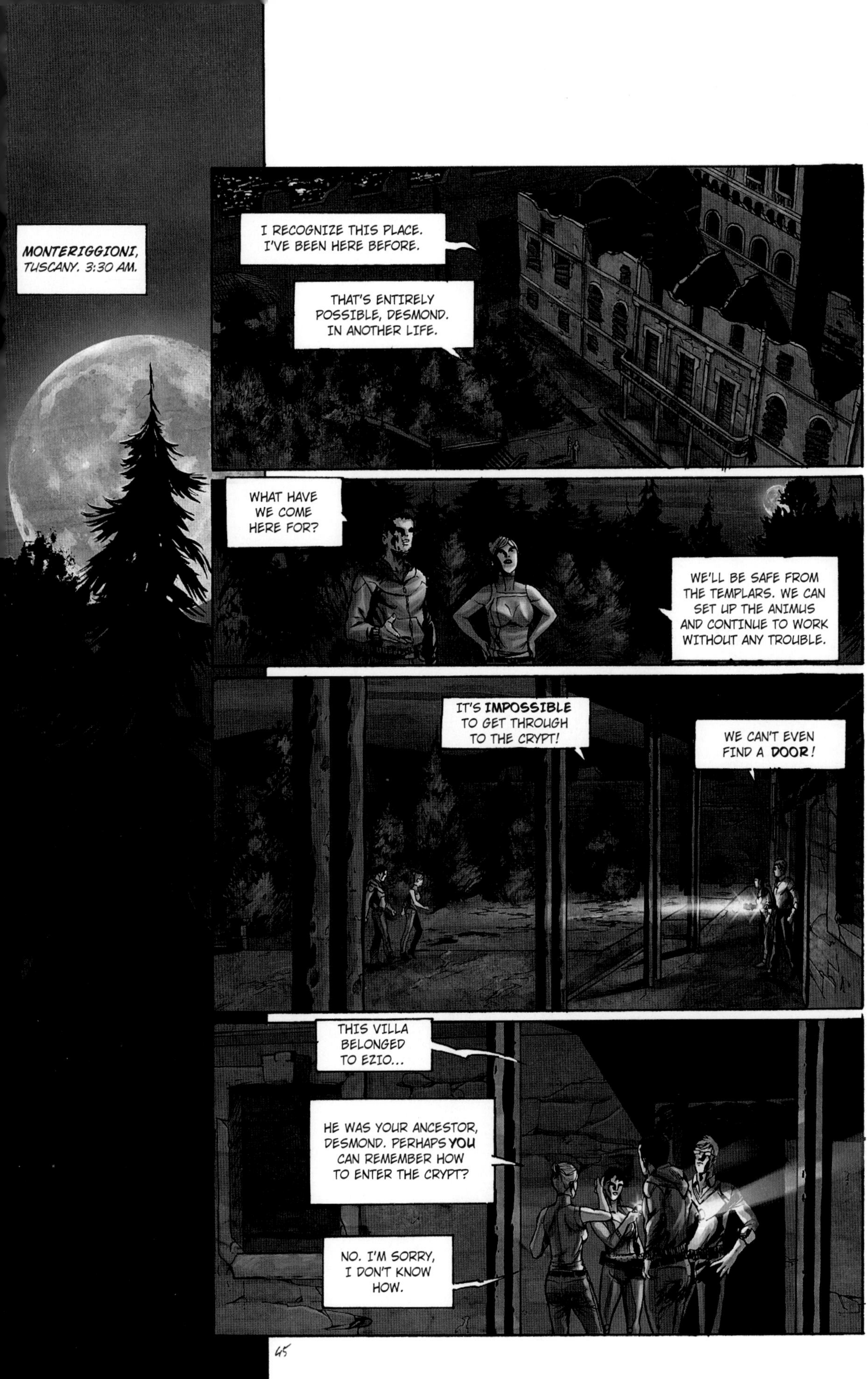
MONTERIGGIONI, TUSCANY. 3:30 AM.
I RECOGNIZE THIS PLACE. I'VE BEEN HERE BEFORE.
THAT'S ENTIRELY POSSIBLE, DESMOND. IN ANOTHER LIFE.
WHAT HAVE WE COME HERE FOR?
WE'LL BE SAFE FROM THE TEMPLARS. WE CAN SET UP THE ANIMUS AND CONTINUE TO WORK WITHOUT ANY TROUBLE.
IT'S **IMPOSSIBLE** TO GET THROUGH TO THE CRYPT!
WE CAN'T EVEN FIND A **DOOR**!
THIS VILLA BELONGED TO EZIO...
HE WAS YOUR ANCESTOR, DESMOND. PERHAPS **YOU** CAN REMEMBER HOW TO ENTER THE CRYPT?
NO. I'M SORRY, I DON'T KNOW HOW.
45

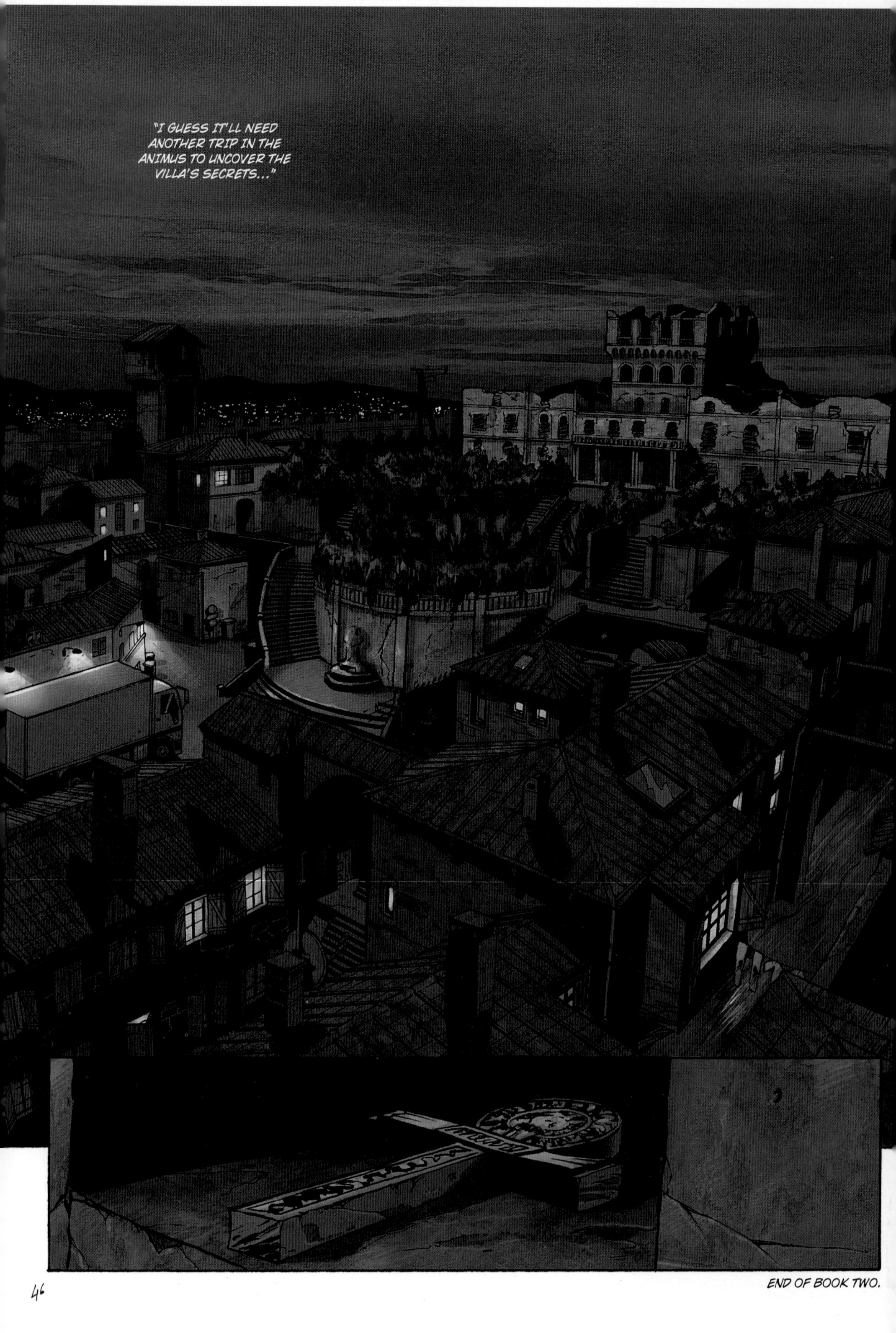
"I GUESS IT'LL NEED ANOTHER TRIP IN THE ANIMUS TO UNCOVER THE VILLA'S SECRETS..."

46

END OF BOOK TWO.